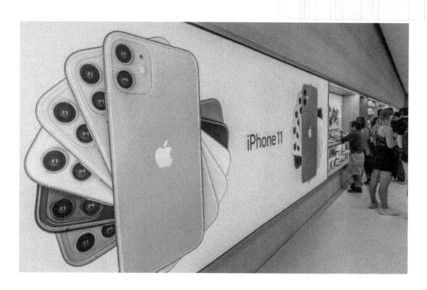

The iPhone 11 Complete User Guide

For Both Veteran and Newbie iPhone Users

Table of Contents

Chapter 1

The New iPhone 11 at a Glance

Every tech-savvy individual living in this fast-paced global village called earth can admit the year 2019 was a great year for the tech industry, and the mobile industry was not left out as it witnessed much growth, improvement, and the shipment of new tech solutions and products. The big giant in the industry – if not the biggest – that is Apple was not left out of the race in technological development. We can also say it is leading the race with its release of high-quality gadgets and devices. In 1984, Apple ventured into revolutionizing personal technology when it introduced the Macintosh computer. Over the years, they have introduced some of the world's most sophisticated and reliable software platforms, such as the macOS, the iOS, tvOS and the watchOS for their Mac devices, as well as iPhones, the Apple TV, and Apple watch. These technological breakthroughs offer their customers a seamless experience across their services, such as the Apple store, iCloud, and Apple music. From MacBooks to iPhones, Apple has been consistent with its ability to match the high aesthetic value in design with optimized functionality. Around mid-2019, the news about the release of the iPhone 11 was all over the internet, and Apple users and fans could not wait to lay their hands on and have a glimpse at the much-anticipated iPhone 11. So, fast forward to the 20th of September 2019; the new iPhone 11 was released in all its glory. Just like the iPhone X and iPhone XR, the new iPhone 11 did not disappoint. iPhone 11 users are surely going to enjoy every cent spent on purchasing this great mobile device, as the seamless integration of optimized hardware and reliable software technologies offer their customers an unparalleled user experience.

Image Credit: apple.com

This revolutionary phone is setting a
new pace as the next big thing in the
iPhone industry, as it is equipped
with many new useful features. It
incorporates amazing new capability
with its top-notch design that the

brand is known for. New additions include the wild and ultra-wide cameras to give your videos and pictures that touch of perfection. The biggest, and what seems to be the greatest addition as it directly affects performance, is the powerful, yet easy to use, iOS 13 operating system. It also comes with the A13 Bionic chip, which Phil Schiller claims to be the fastest chip ever installed in a smartphone. (If you're wondering who Phil Schiller is, he is the senior vice president of worldwide marketing at Apple.) Because people want to get things done as quickly as possible, you wouldn't want to be wielding a good-looking but inadequate phone that takes forever to load certain apps and to accomplish your daily tasks. The A13 Bionic chip ensures your everyday tasks are handled efficiently.

This book will provide you with tips and information on what to expect from your new iPhone 11 and how to use most of its major features.

Chapter 2

Buying the New iPhone 11

On September 10, the news of the launch of iPhone 11 took the internet by storm, and just a few days after the launch, the device was released on the 20th of September. The much-awaited iPhone comes in six beautiful colours and at a reasonable price of 699 US dollars. Almost every important feature you can think of as necessary for your everyday tasks has been improved, including improved battery life to last you throughout the entire day with just a single charge, a water-resistant design, and an upgraded chip to help with some of the most demanding tasks iPhone users want to perform. The most talked-about feature – the dual-camera system – is intuitive and promises to give users an exceptional video and photo experience during the day and at night, as the performance of the night mode feature seems to have been improved massively.

The iPhone 11 is available in memory size models of 64GB, 128GB, and 256GB.

As usual, it ships in the two major colours, black and white, for most phones. You can also choose from four other beautiful colours to match your personality, i.e., purple, yellow, green, and flashy red. The 128GB model is priced at 749 US dollars, and the 256GB model sells for 849 US dollars. Earlier iPhone customers can acquire the iPhone 11 through the iPhone Upgrade Program, with a monthly payment of about 29 US dollars per month for the 64GB model, while the 128GB version can be acquired with a monthly payment of about 31 US dollars. If you want the 256GB model, then you should be willing to pay about 35 US dollars monthly for it. Apple customers in the United States and more than 30 other countries can purchase the iPhone 11 from an approved Apple authorized reseller after the 20th of September.

All new iPhone 11 customers who make a direct purchase from Apple are offered free personal setup in the Apple store. This includes helping you to erase data from the old device, transfer useful data into your new device, set up user accounts such as your email and provide you with useful tips on how to make the most out of the new features. If you choose to buy your iPhone 11 from the Apple store using the Apple card, you get 3 per cent daily cash. You can also extend your limited warranty using AppleCare+, which would give you 24 hours a day and 7 days a week access to their technical support team, with priority access.

There are many platforms where you can learn more about the new iPhone 11, but the new Today at Apple session is the major Apple platform where you can leverage on a 15-minute drop-in session to learn quick tips and tricks on how to maximize the capabilities of the iPhone 11. The session covers interesting topics such as photography and video recording/videography using your iPhone.

Chapter 3

Deep Dive Into the iPhone 11 Design

About a year after releasing the iPhone XR, which received a high level of acceptability within the Apple user's community, the big tech giant went ahead to release yet another device that completes the checklist of important features for a great mobile device. The new iPhone 11 features the Liquid Retina High Definition Display, which is a 6.1-inch LCD display. This comes with a maximum brightness value of 625 nits, a contrast ratio of 1400:1, and a resolution of 1792 by 828 at 326ppi. This makes it a great mobile device for taking quality photos that are sharp and clear enough to reveal minute details when zoomed in closely. The true tone support feature gives your images that extra touch of professionalism when properly used to adjust the white balance to the ambient lighting.

Image Credit: apple.com

The iPhone 11 has a glass body design that comes in six different colours: white, yellow, purple, green and red, with the purple and green being new colour additions to the iPhone brands in 2019. It appears the millennials are beginning to have some say in the design of Apple products or someone in charge of that decision-making process is conquering his fear of colours. Whatever the case may be, I can certainly see this as a step in the right direction for the big tech giant, as it will rule out one edge some other brands have over them, even though we know the iPhone brand is uniquely set apart from other mobile phone brands. Although the iPhone 11 does not come with 3D Touch, like the iPhone XR, it incorporates Haptic Touch, which is also efficient, and the iOS 13 platform supports Haptic Touch, even though it lacks that much-needed pressure sensitivity of the 3D touch.

Looking at the iPhone 11 and comparing it with the iPhone XR, you might not spot much difference except for the dual camera in iPhone 11, but when it comes to design criteria, the iPhone 11 is miles ahead of the iPhone XR. The iPhone 11 is constructed of glass material that is said to be the toughest glass ever used in making a smartphone. This boosts the overall durability of the iPhone 11 and offers improved water resistance. According to Apple, the iPhone 11 was tested by professionals under controlled lab conditions at a maximum depth of 2 meters for about 30 minutes, i.e., at a rating of IP68 based on the IEC standard 60529. Although this test confirms the iPhone 11 to be splash, dust and water-resistant, you should also be aware that the splash, water and dust resistance test was performed within timeframes and that continuous exposure of your device to such conditions will decrease its ability to resist these substances over time due to the effect of wear. So, don't go take a swim with your iPhone just because it is water-resistant. You should also take note that Apple won't cater to liquid damage as it is not covered under the warranty. If your phone gets submerged in water, make sure you dry it properly before usage. You can always refer to the instructions on the user guide for cleaning tips. Also, do not attempt to charge your iPhone when it gets wet.

Let's explore some features of the iPhone 11 camera. The dual-lens camera is the most visible feature that sets the iPhone 11 apart from the iPhone

XR. This introduction is a great improvement over the single-lens camera. It offers you the standard wide-angle shot camera settings and then the new ultra-wide-angle camera setting that offers you a 120-degree field of view. That is indeed an amazing feature for those who would love to use their iPhone 11 for taking sharp and colourful pictures that are so realistic and show a great level of details when zoomed. Although the telephoto lens of the iPhone 11 Pro and Pro Max are not available for the iPhone 11, the dual-lens camera – when used properly – can still give you a great output, so be sure to check out the guides on how to get the best out of your iPhone 11 camera.

Unlike the iPhone XR that only supports portrait mode for person shots, the iPhone 11 has been upgraded to support different portrait mode shots. This means you can set up both the wide and ultra-wide cameras to shoot portraits of pets, people, your laptop or any other object you might want to capture in memory. The ultra-wide-angle camera's exceptional ability is not limited to taking selfies and images of your cats; it is also ideal for taking nature photos, so don't limit your adventure. Apple claims the ultra-wide lens can capture up to four times more scenery than the conventional single-lens camera, so using it for landscape photoshoots and architectural shots isn't such a bad idea.

The simple principle behind the exceptional ability of the ultra-wide camera is that the camera interface of the iPhone 11 was upgraded with devices that offer you a more immersive experience, so you can see beyond the boundaries of your frame. This is complemented with the 2x optical zoom and supported with the digital zoom up to 5x.

Have you always envied the Google Pixel device because of its Night Sight mode that allows you to take some pretty cool photos at night? Well, if you get the new iPhone 11, you won't have any reason to desire the night mode camera ability of the Google Pixel devices. Apple has provided its customers with an improved Night Mode feature in the iPhone 11 with great capabilities to process good quality images within a low lighting environment. The ultra-wide range camera lens and the night mode feature will combine to produce a crisp, clear photo at night.

Within the information technology industry, the next big thing is artificial intelligence and machine learning. The big tech industries and institutions are exploring ways to improve their products and services by leveraging on the huge advantage artificial intelligence and machine learning have to offer. Therefore, we seeing self-driven cars and more jobs becoming automated through artificial intelligence. Apple has found a way to integrate machine learning into the iPhone, as the Smart HDR leverages on the machine learning ability to capture natural-looking images and improve features that give images a touch of realism, such as a high level of shadow and highlight detailing. The iOS 13.2 has been developed with a Deep Fusion technology that takes advantage of machine learning technology in pixel by pixel processing of your pictures. This offers users of the iPhone 11 a better photographic experience as the textures are optimized, while background noise and grains are minimized. Generally, compared to the iPhone XR, photos taken by the iPhone 11 are much more detailed and, to a large extent, depend the photographic skill of the user.

A lot of people love making videos using their iPhones. It is almost becoming a trend these days, as a considerable number of vloggers rely on their iPhones to create amazing and engaging content across various platforms. When a professional makes a video using a good iPhone, like the iPhone 11 or iPhone 11 Pro, you would hardly believe it was shot using a mobile device. This gives users the advantage of carrying a powerful camera on their mobile device wherever they go. The 4K video recording is improved with an extended dynamic range of sixty (60), thirty (30) and twenty (20) frames per second (fps). You can also make your video recordings using both the single lens and the dual-lens cameras. If you begin with one and want to switch to the other, you can easily do that by simply tapping on your screen through the live swapping property. With the QuickTake video feature, you can press the camera app shutter button to track your subject while video recording, while the Audio Zoom feature helps to produce more dynamic sound by matching the audio with the video framing. The new iPhone 11 also supports the Dolby Atmos sound system and is built with the new spatial audio feature that is specially designed to simulate the surrounding sound to offer the user a more immersive sound experience. All these technologies put together offer you a great sound output that you can hardly get in any other mobile device.

The new improved features in the iPhone 11 are also taking "slofies" to an entirely new level with the front-facing TrueDepth camera setting that supports 120 frames per second slow motion video for the first time. So, you can enjoy taking slow motions selfies and adding Hollywood styled slow motion touch to your videos. This ability to capture slow motion is due to the upgrade of the iPhone 11 TrueDepth camera, with a whopping 12-megapixel camera that increased the efficiency of the Face ID, with up to 30 per cent increase in speed and the ability to capture images from more angles. With the true depth camera, you can have more natural and realistic looking images as it supports the next generation smart HDR and can record 4k videos at a frame rate of 60 fps.

The iPhone 11 looks like the iPhone XR in many ways, but there are physical changes in design that you can spot when you compare the phones. The iPhone 11, just like the iPhone XR, is designed with a 7000 series aluminium frame that is machined to precision. This aluminium material covers the phone's glass enclosure. At 6.1 inches, the display dimension of the iPhone 11 is a little greater than the iPhone Pro's display dimension, which is at 5.8 inches, while the iPhone 11 Pro Max has a higher display dimension of 6.5 inches. More comparisons between the iPhone 11 and other devices will be discussed later in the book.

The iPhone 11 is an all display mobile device, except for the speaker, ambient lighting, and Face ID camera notch. There are no home buttons on the iPhone 11. It has an edge to edge display that is complemented by a slim bezel and a notch installed at the top to operate the TrueDepth camera system. Since the iPhone uses the LCD display in place of the OLED display, the bezels are a little thicker than that of the iPhone 11 Pro and Prom Max models.

Like many other iPhone designs, Apple has maintained the portability of iPhones in the design of the iPhone 11. The new iPhone 11 weighs around 6.84 ounces, almost the same weight as the iPhone XR. This weight reflects good material design capabilities within the iPhone's hardware engineering department, as they have found a way to integrate the lightweight but effective hardware devices into the design of the iPhone 11. This makes the phone ideal for everyone, as you can simply drop it into your pocket without feeling like you are carrying a dumbbell in your pocket. The dimensioning is also key to its portability as it measures about 150.9 mm in height, 75.7 mm in width, and it has a thickness of about

8.3 mm. This dimension is identical to that of the iPhone XR, while the thickness is higher than that of the iPhone 11 Pro and iPhone 11 Pro Max by 0.2 mm.

If you're an iPhone XR user and you take a first glance at the iPhone 11, you will notice one major difference when you turn the phone to its back, and that is the camera. The new square-shaped dual-lens camera could be said to be the design ace up the sleeve of the Apple company before the release of the iPhone 11. The dual-lens camera is enclosed with a square-shaped bump that gradually flows into the rest of the phone casing. Since the camera elements are thicker than the phone body, the dual lenses protrude from the body of the phone, but this slight bulge adds to the aesthetic appeal of the iPhone as it blends smoothly into the surface. Another major change you will notice when you look closely is with the Apple logo. The Apple logo's position has been changed from the usual top corner and has been moved to the centre of the phone. Most reviewers are of the opinion that this change in design is due to the planned implementation of a two-charging system feature that did not get implemented. Had this new two-way design feature been successful, this would mean the iPhone 11 would have a bilateral wireless charging system that would power other apple devices, such as the Apple Air pods and the Apple Watch.

The last design feature noted in this chapter is the durable glass material of the iPhone. This was designed using what Apple calls the dual ion-exchange process. For those of us who have no background in chemistry or material design, it simply means the result is a stronger glass material that protects both the front and the back of the iPhone 11. According to Apple, it is the most durable material used for a smartphone, meaning better durability and an ability to withstand accidental drops and adhesion against some surfaces. But you should also handle it with care, as it is still glass. To secure your iPhone 11, it is advisable to get a matching case for your phone. The paddings provided by such cases offer a lot of protection to your phone by damping out the effect of bumps and falls. You should also get AppleCare+ in case you experience accidental damage to your iPhone. We will explain some of the requirements and details of AppleCare+ in the next chapter.

Chapter 4

Everything You Need to Know About Apple Care and Apple Care +

There are those of us who are just too clumsy and are most likely to drop things, even our mobile phones, mistakenly. Well, you don't have to feel bad or blame yourself because that is a mistake most people make occasionally. But even though you shouldn't feel bad about it, there is serious cause for concern when you purchase the iPhone 11, worth over 600 US dollar. That is why Apple introduced the Apple Care phone warranty plans. Those of you who don't know much about Apple Care may be asking questions such as, what exactly is this AppleCare+? Is it necessary for all iPhone users, and if so, what makes it so important?

Image Credit: Phone Arena

What is Apple Care and AppleCare+?

To begin with, Apple Care and AppleCare+ are not the same thing, although most iPhone users are fond of interchanging the words, thinking they mean the same thing. That plus sign that differentiates them indicates a huge difference in coverages. So, let's get down to the bottom of both coverages.

Apple Care is termed the Limited Warranty Coverage by Apple. Apple Care is what everyone gets when he or she purchases any Apple product. It is not limited to iPhone devices, but it includes all Apple Watches, Air pod devices, the Apple TV, and even MacBooks. You can call it the baseline warranty coverage for purchasing any new Apple product. On the other hand, the AppleCare+ is not free for all iPhone customers; it is an add-on service that is paid for.

Just like with every other mobile phone brand or product manufacturer, the warranty is a form of fault or damage coverage given to the customer. This is a guarantee that the device or product is expected to work well within a specific timeframe without developing any fault in functionality. If anything goes wrong with the device within that period and it was no fault of the user, the manufacturer takes the responsibility of fixing the device and returning it to a functional state at no cost to the customer. So, Apple Care is simply a product warranty with a fancy name. Since Apple is a company that produces both hardware and operating systems that are truly integrated across various products, only Apple Care or AppleCare+ can afford you access to experts who offer you a one-stop solution to your iPhone issues.

Features and Benefits Surrounding the Apple Care Warranty

Like most manufacturers, the length of coverage is within a set time limit after which the company signs off taking such responsibilities. For Apple, there is usually a one-year warranty on all their products. This warranty covers any form of damage or breakage that is no fault of the customer or the iPhone user in this case. So, complaints like the power button randomly stopped working, the mouthpiece seems to be faulty, or some factory-installed software seems not to work as it should, would all be entertained within that period. But if you drop your phone and the screen shatters, such damages are not going to be covered even for a single day after purchasing your iPhone, as it would be deemed a user fault damage.

The Apple Care warranty is also transferrable from one user to another. This means that, if you buy an Apple device and decide to resell to someone else, the new user would enjoy the remaining warranty period. For example, if you purchase the iPhone 11 and then decide to resell it to another user after five (5) months of usage, the Apple Care coverage would automatically be transferred to the new user to enjoy the remaining seven (7) months of coverage on the device.

The Apple Care warranty is applicable to all Apple devices irrespective of where you purchased them, so far as they are certified distributors of the device. This means that, even if you bought your iPhone 11 from Amazon or from XYZ store, you would get the complete Apple Care coverage and all its benefits as though you purchased your iPhone directly from an Apple store.

Features and Benefits Surrounding the AppleCare+ Warranty

Now we understand all about Apple Care warranty coverage and what all Apple customers stand to benefit when they make a purchase. So, what happens when you want an extra warranty or coverage for your iPhone, in case you accidentally bump it against a hard surface or it drops? You would simply opt-in for the AppleCare+ coverage that is available for those who simply want to extend their warranty coverage timeframe from one year to two years. This means that whatever fault your iPhone develops within the period of two years that is not a result of a mistake on your own part would be taken care of by Apple. If you also want to add extra coverage to your free 1-year warranty, such as the glass screen shattering as a result of your iPhone dropping, you can do that with the AppleCare+ warranty coverage plan.

To enjoy the accidental damage coverage of AppleCare+, you simply pay a fee to upgrade from Apple Care to AppleCare+. This payment is based on the Apple device you purchased, be it an iPhone, an Apple Watch or a MacBook. This upgrade can come in handy as most accidental damages would cost you more than the payment for the AppleCare+ subscription.

Let me take you through a quick rundown on the cost of AppleCare+ coverage on some Apple devices. The information provided below is the coverage fees for Apple products as discovered through detailed research and survey. The information provided is to let you know what you should expect the coverage fee to be, but they are subject to changes by Apple.

The iPhone 11, iPhone 11 Pro, iPhone XS, iPhone XS Max and iPhone X coverage fees are set at 199 US dollar. The fee for iPhone XR, iPhone 8 Plus and iPhone 7 Plus is 149 US dollar, while that of the iPhone 8 and iPhone 7 is 129 dollars. For the MacBook and MacBook Air, you can get coverage at 269 dollars, while coverage for the 13-inch and 15-inch MacBook Pro goes for 269 and 379 US dollars, respectively. For the Apple Watch series, the coverage fee for series 4 is set at 79 dollars, while that of series 3 is at 49 dollars. The coverage for iMac is 169 dollars and the Mac Mini is 99 dollars. The Apple TV and Home Pod have a coverage fee of 29 and 30 dollars, respectively.

Paying for these coverages does not automatically mean you can take your phone for repair no matter how many times it gets damaged as a result of an accidental drop or scratch. You should read through the terms and conditions as provided by Apple. Most times, you are likely to get only two incidents of accidental coverage if it is your fault, and there are deductibles per device as well. For any iPhone model, the deductible for any form of screen damage is 29 dollars, while damages other than screen breakage are 99 dollars. For the MacBook series, the screen damage deductible is 99 dollars, while other forms of damage are 299 dollars. For the iPod Touch, the Home Pod and the Apple Watch, the deductibles for any form of damage is 29 dollars, 39 dollars, and 69 dollars, respectively.

Another form of useful coverage AppleCare+ provides is coverage for theft or loss. Enrolling in this coverage allows you to replace a lost or stolen iPhone. To get this coverage, you have to pay an extra fee in addition to the AppleCare+ coverage fee for each iPhone device. For the iPhone 7 and iPhone 8, the fee is an extra 800 dollars, while every other later iPhone version, i.e., the iPhone X series and iPhone 11 series, is set at an extra 100 dollars.

Just like the regular AppleCare+ coverage has deductibles, there are deductibles for the AppleCare+ theft and loss coverage. The deductibles for the iPhone 6, 6S, 7 and 8 is 199 dollars, while that of the iPhone XR, 8 Plus, 6S Plus and 7 Plus is fixed at 229 dollars. For the iPhone X, the XS, and XS Max, the deductible is 269 dollars, and the iPhone 11 Pro and iPhone 11 Pro Max is 299 dollars.

Having to pay for deductibles and AppleCare+ after purchasing an expensive iPhone is not so desirable. But the cushion effects it would have in the event of any damage or loss of your iPhone would be substantial. Imagine losing your iPhone 11 and having to spend about 269 dollars for a replacement, rather than the full cost of a new iPhone 11. You would be saving over 400 dollars in that process. The question of whether you should get AppleCare+ is entirely up to you and depends on how you use your iPhone. If you know you are prone to dropping your phone or bumping it against hard surfaces, you should consider getting AppleCare+ coverage, and if you are forgetful, like so many should read through the terms and conditions as provided by Apple. Most times, you are likely to get only two incidents of accidental coverage if it is your fault, and there are deductibles per device as well. For any iPhone model, the deductible for any form of screen damage is 29 dollars, while damages other than screen breakage are 99 dollars. For the MacBook series, the screen damage deductible is 99 dollars, while other forms of damage are 299 dollars. For the iPod Touch, the Home Pod and the Apple Watch, the deductibles for any form of damage is 29 dollars, 39 dollars, and 69 dollars, respectively.

Another form of useful coverage AppleCare+ provides is coverage for theft or loss. Enrolling in this coverage allows you to replace a lost or stolen iPhone. To get this coverage, you have to pay an extra fee in addition to the AppleCare+ coverage fee for each iPhone device. For the iPhone 7 and iPhone 8, the fee is an extra 800 dollars, while every other later iPhone version, i.e., the iPhone X series and iPhone 11 series, is set at an extra 100 dollars.

Just like the regular AppleCare+ coverage has deductibles, there are deductibles for the AppleCare+ theft and loss coverage. The deductibles for the iPhone 6, 6S, 7 and 8 is 199 dollars, while that of the iPhone XR, 8 Plus, 6S Plus and 7 Plus is fixed at 229 dollars. For the iPhone X, the XS, and XS Max, the deductible is 269 dollars, and the iPhone 11 Pro and iPhone 11 Pro Max is 299 dollars.

Having to pay for deductibles and AppleCare+ after purchasing an expensive iPhone is not so desirable. But the cushion effects it would have in the event of any damage or loss of your iPhone would be substantial. Imagine losing your iPhone 11 and having to spend about 269 dollars for a replacement, rather than the full cost of a new iPhone 11. You would be saving over 400 dollars in that process. The question of whether you should get AppleCare+ is entirely up to you and depends on how you use your iPhone. If you know you are prone to dropping your phone or bumping it against hard surfaces, you should consider getting AppleCare+ coverage, and if you are forgetful, like so many other individuals who deal with many activities in a fast-paced environment, you should consider getting AppleCare+ Theft and Loss coverage, as that extra coverage fee could save you a lot of money when something eventually happens. You can take it as a form of "phone insurance". One other thing you stand to benefit is peace of mind; you are assured that you have your iPhone covered. Whatever the case may be, whether you're getting AppleCare+ or AppleCare+ with Theft and Loss, you should ensure you handle your device properly and always keep it safe to avoid loss. It is better to be on the safer side by reading through all the terms and conditions of the AppleCare+ coverage, so you know what is applicable.

For Apple Theft and Loss coverage, at the time of theft or misplacement of your iPhone, you are required to have the Find My iPhone feature enabled on your iPhone, although there may be certain exclusions from this. It is also important to ensure your iPhone is associated with your Apple ID during that process because the process of getting you a new iPhone includes erasing the information on your missing iPhone, disabling it, and transferring ownership to your newly issued device. Ensure you remember your Apple ID and password, as you would need that to sign in to your Find My iPhone account, so make sure you always keep your account information up to date. You can also add an extra level of security by using the two-factor authentication login for your Apple ID, but if you do this, it is also recommended you link your account to another trusted phone number that you can receive the secured six-digit verification code needed to sign in to your account if you lose your iPhone.

How to Buy Coverage for your iPhone 11

You can purchase coverage immediately when you buy your iPhone 11, or you can buy it within 60 days of purchasing your phone. To set it up, turn on your device and go to *Settings*, then select the *General* settings tab and open the *About* phone section and choose the AppleCare+ coverage. You can also use the online support platform to chat with a customer support agent, who will lead you through the entire process. Last, you can decide to visit an Apple store close to you. For the last two options, it is required you have your serial number and proof of purchase as diagnostics and inspection will be carried out on your phone.

How to Contact Apple to Kickstart your AppleCare+ Coverage Benefits

If you need any form of repair or replacement, there are various ways you can reach out to the customer support team. As an Apple customer with an AppleCare+ coverage plan, you have 24 hours a day and 7 days a week priority access to their customer support experts, and if you stay in any metropolitan area around the world, you can be assured of getting same day service.

You also have express replacement service, so you will spend minimal time without an iPhone, as a replacement will be shipped to you, so you don't have to wait for the repair. I will explain more about the express replacement service shortly.

You can send your iPhone to Apple by mailing it in using the Apple prepaid shipping box, or you can use the Carry-in repair method by taking your iPhone to the nearest Apple-authorized service provider.

AppleCare+ Express Replacement Service is available for your iPhone 11

This feature is a benefit enjoyed by Apple customers who acquire AppleCare+ coverage. When you request express replacement, Apple sends you a replacement for your iPhone 11 immediately, as well as packaging to help you return your damaged phone for proper repairs.

The Cost of Express Replacement Service

When you order express replacement service using your AppleCare+ coverage plan, you only have to pay for the replacement service, as Apple covers the express delivery for you. As explained earlier, all rules guiding the AppleCare+ and Apple Care also apply to the express replacement service. So, if you're requesting a repair that is not a result of an accident and your warranty period has not elapsed and you request express replacement service, you need not pay any fee.

How to Return Your Original iPhone

Once you request express replacement service, a new iPhone will be shipped to you with factory settings and other necessary information. You are to return your original iPhone to Apple within 10 working days of requesting a replacement to avoid paying late fees. Usually, when you request express replacement service, you permit a temporary authorization on your credit card. This covers the complete replacement value of your iPhone and becomes invalid or expires if your repair issue is covered under the normal Apple Care warranty and you send back your original product with the specified 10 business days. If you fail to send your damaged iPhone to Apple within 10 business days after you receive the replacement or you did send it but Apple never received it, you will be charged the full replacement amount, and this will be deducted from your card. If your phone arrives late and the fault is covered under warranty, then the replacement value initially deducted will be refunded to your account and only the late fee will be charged.

Replacement Amounts and Late Fees for iPhone 11

Here are the corresponding replacement values and late fees for iPhone 11, iPhone 11 Pro and iPhone 11 Pro Max.

iPhone 11 64 GB, 128 GB and 256 GB all have a replacement value of $ 699, $ 749 and $ 849, respectively, while their late fee is $ 150, $ 175 and $ 225, respectively.

iPhone 11 Pro 64 GB, 128 GB and 256 GB all have a replacement value of $ 999, $ 1,149 and $ 1,349, respectively, while their late fee is $ 225, $ 300 and $400, respectively.

iPhone 11 Pro Max 64 GB, 128 GB and 256 GB all have a replacement value of $ 1,099, $ 1,249 and $ 1,449, respectively, while their late fee is $ 250, $ 325 and $425, respectively.

Renewing Your AppleCare+ Coverage

Once your AppleCare+ initial yearly coverage expires, you can renew or subscribe to a more flexible monthly plan. For example, if you subscribed to an initial 24- or 36-month coverage and this time elapses, you can switch to a monthly basis coverage payment. The monthly plan renews automatically until you cancel the plan. Once your first coverage of 24 or 36 months ends, you can no longer subscribe to a yearly plan, only the monthly plan. To check your coverage status, you can log in to mysupport.apple.com using your Apple ID and selecting your device. Another option is for you to open the Apple support app on your iPhone 11. Then sign in to your account and tap on Check Coverage.

Chapter 5

The Powerful iPhone 11 Processor

At Apple's annual event when the iPhone is launched, the vice president of silicon engineering at Apple, Sri Santhanam, said the chip for the new iPhone 11, the iPhone 11 Pro, and the iPhone 11 Pro Max is the highest performing chip ever built for their iPhones. When compared to previous iPhones processors, the new A13 is said to boost performance by at least 20 per cent. This upgrade includes the main processor and other engines that support the AI and graphics display.

Image Credit: Techtalk.vn

The design of this new iPhone saw a massive increase in the number of transistors used for an iPhone. From the 6.9 billion transistors of the previous year, the new iPhone 11, iPhone 11 Pro and Pro Max are composed of a total of 8.6 billion transistors. The function of transistors in a mobile device or any other computer device is essential, as it is the fundamental component that determines the processing power of your computer chips. The more of them you have, the more efficiently you can execute your tasks. Your phone apps begin to speed up and experience no lag, and your graphics display is also improved.

The new iPhone 11 processor is an A13 bionic 7-nanometer chip that comes with a third generation neural engine . The previous version used in the iPhone X series, A12, was at a lower performance rate of 20 per cent compared to the new A13 processor. This improvement is not limited to the CPU; the GPU has improved in its efficiency as well. These improvements in performance are largely due to the new machine learning accelerators introduced to increase the efficiency of the CPU, as it can now perform over 1 trillion operations within a second. This improvement in efficiency has also increased the neural engine speed in processing graphical related functions on the iPhone, such as improving the video display, giving users a better gaming experience by preventing gaming lags, and improving the real-time photography experience by giving you clearer snapshots and selfies with as many details as possible.

Since Apple designs its own chips, it can optimize their designs, meaning they can determine how to integrate their chips to form an efficient package; this way, silicon valley estates can be mapped out for specific tasks such as improving the graphics and AI, prioritizing user experience design, and reducing power consumption. This advantage of running the entire production stack is a key component in the huge success behind the A13 processing power, as it allows them to maintain a steady performance advantage over other top-end Android phone processors. Even most smartphones are part of the ARM processor family.

In the early days of manufacturing microprocessors, improving chips was a lot trickier than it is now, as present chip makers are constantly looking for ways to shrink transistors to smaller sizes while coming up with more efficient designs. This usually comes at a high cost of manufacturing. To achieve this efficiency, they apply to work with the Taiwan Semiconductor Manufacturing Corporation TSMC to build smaller high-performance chips. The Taiwan Semiconductor Manufacturing company employs new techniques to enhance them, including miniaturizing them and coupling memory in a tighter way to improve overall performance.

The great reduction in the size of the iPhone chip started remarkably with the A12 processor, which was used for the iPhone XS, the iPhone XR and the iPhone XS Max. These Apple mobile devices were the first to be built using the Taiwan Semiconductor Manufacturing Corporation's second-generation 7-nanometer manufacturing process. To understand or have an idea of how deep their manufacturing process and chip miniaturization is, let us compare that to the size of a virus, which is about 50 nanometer in width. Manufacturing a chip that small is quite remarkable, as it requires a lot of technical expertise in manufacturing. According to Sri Santhanam, the A13 processor's second-generation 7-nanometer manufacturing process produced a chip that is more powerful and efficient even at the reduced size. The main A13 processor comes with four smaller processors to handle low-power processing, such as background tasks. This takes the load off your battery, so it lasts longer. Sri Santhanam also noted that the power consumption of all engines was reduced by a whopping 40 per cent. With the improvement in battery life, the iPhone 11 lasts one extra hour when subjected to the same battery load as the iPhone XR. You can enjoy at least 10 hours of watching your favourite movies and videos on your iPhone, as it allows up to 17 hours of video playback from the device memory and supports at least 10 hours of video streaming. You can enjoy listening to your favourite artist tracks for hours with audio playback of 65 hours. The iPhone 11 comes with the standard 5W charger and, like the iPhone 11 Pro and iPhone 11 Pro Max, the iPhone 11 enables fast charging, although this requires extra charging equipment.

The iPhone 11 is designed with an Intel modem chip in the Gigabit-class LTE. Other features include a 2x2 MIMO and LAA, a Bluetooth 5.0 and Wi-Fi 6 support (802.11 ax) feature. Included also is a dual SIM slot with the eSIM option and the U1 ultra-wideband chip to improve spatial awareness and enable better indoor tracking. With the iOS 13.1 chip design, the iPhone has been improved through machine learning to suggest directions for Airdrops. This simply means you can point your phone to any other iPhone user you want to share files with, and Airdrop will do the rest.

In later chapters, we will review more changes in design and platform performance between the previous iPhone X series and the iPhone 11 family.

Chapter 6

Setting Up Your New iPhone 11

So, your iPhone just arrived and it's fresh out of the box. You begin to ask yourself: "What do I do next?" Well, I have you covered, as I am going to breakdown the first things you should do with your iPhone to get it set up for you to enjoy.

Step One – Turn on Your Phone

The first thing you should do after getting your new iPhone 11 is get rid of your previous phone. Yeah, you can just throw it in the thrash – just kidding. Before you discard your old phone, just know there are safety measures you need to follow to ensure that your information is safe. We will discuss this in a later chapter. Now, back to the first step in setting up your new iPhone. Getting rid of your previous phone means turning it off because the aim of setting up the new one is to move your information from your previous iPhone to the new one.

Once you're sure you've turned off your old iPhone, the next thing you need to do is power on your new iPhone 11. This is quite straight forward; all you need to do is locate the power button on the right side of the phone. Then press it down until the Apple logo appears then let go of the pressure. The phone should boot up in no time with its improved processor. Once the phone comes up, you can take a deep breath and behold it in all its awesomeness.

Step Two - Choose Your Preferred Language and Location

When the phone turns on successfully, you should be greeted by a welcome screen. Slide up this screen to start your configuration. The next thing is to select the English language and your country of residence. I am assuming English is your language of choice, as these instructions are in English. You can select your preferred language and proceed with the next step but know that, from this point, your choice of language affects everything on your phone, including date, time, calendar and contacts. After selecting your preferred language, choose your country or region.

Step Three – Setting Up Your Accessibility Option

The next step is to set up your accessibility option. Simply tap on the blue accessibility button to continue. If you don't find these next steps necessary, you can jump to the next step on launching the QuickStart.

Step Four – Using the Quick Start

Apple has made setting up the Quick Start as easy as possible for iPhone users with iOS 11 platform and above. If you are using an iPhone with an iOS 13 or later platform, such as the iPhone 11 with an iOS 13 platform, all you need to do is bring the two phones together to begin the automatic set up. If you have any iPhone with an earlier iOS, you have to use the manual set up. To access this, tap on the Set Up Manually button.

Step Five – Activating Your Device

To activate your phone, make sure your SIM card is on your iPhone, as you need to connect to the Wi-Fi or any other network service. Tap on the available Wi-Fi you want to connect with to get started.

Step Six - Setting up FACE ID or Touch ID

The Face ID and Touch ID are the key settings that offer you a good level of security on your iPhone, so it is one of the first things you should set up when you unpack your iPhone 11. The Face ID and Touch ID security are used when you want to unlock your iPhone 11 or make online store purchases or other forms of transactions. When the Face ID option comes up, simply tap on the continue button to proceed and set up your Face ID or tap Set Up Later in Settings if you intend to do it later. Once you tap Continue, you will be prompted to enter a passcode; this ensures your Face ID or Touch ID is not changed without your permission. Enter your six-digit passcode to secure your data and provide you alone with the ability to unlock your iPhone 11. If you would like a custom code or you want a four-digit code, tap on the Passcode Options. (You will also get the option of using no passcode at all). But be aware that your iPhone 11 is more secure with your passcode. It is better to use a supposedly simple passcode than no passcode at all. I have provided more information on the Apple Face ID and Touch ID in the following chapters.

Step Seven – Transferring Your Information and Restoring Data from Old Devices

From the Apps and Data section, you can retrieve your data from your iCloud and iTunes account backup into your new iPhone 11. You have the option to restore from your iCloud Backup, your Mac or PC, to transfer directly from iPhone, to Move Data from Android. If there are no backups for you to transfer into your iPhone 11, select the Set Up as New device option to proceed. You can read more informative tips and procedures on data transfer and migration on your iPhone 11 in subsequent chapters.

Step Eight – Login with Your Apple ID

On the Apple ID page, you have the option to sign in with your Apple ID to use iCloud, iTunes, and other Apps from the App store. Enter your Apple ID and continue or tap on the Forgot Password button to retrieve your Apple ID and password. Don't have an Apple ID? You can use Don't Have an Apple ID tab to create your own Apple ID. For users with their Apple ID's signed into other devices, you might be prompted to enter a verification code from your older iPhone. If you use more than a single Apple ID across your Apple Accounts, you can use the Use Different Apple IDs for iTunes and iClouds to login with the proper Apple ID into the separate accounts.

Step Nine – Allowing Automatic Updates

When you continue allowing the automatic updates, you will get the latest features and security updates. You will be notified automatically of any improvements or iOS upgrades. If you do not want to share your information with app developers by turning on automatic updates, you can choose the Install Updates Manually, so you can decide when to check your iPhone for new apps and iOS upgrades. Turning on the automatic updates does not mean you won't have any restrictions on the installation of the updates. Before any update is installed, you will be sent a notification, and you can choose to allow updates or discontinue the automatic updates from the Settings.

Step Ten - Time to Put Siri to Work

Siri is the Apple AI that will serve as your device assistant. You just say Hi Siri or press on the side button to get Siri to work, as Siri is willing to help you get things done if you ask. Simply press the Continue button and follow the instructions to complete the setup. You might need to say a few words or phrases, so you and Siri can get to know each other, as Siri works better when it knows its owner's voice.

Step Eleven - Configure the Screen Time

With the Screen Time configuration, you can get a weekly report to give you insights on how much screen time you or your kids spend on your iPhone. You can also manage your apps by setting time limits and parental controls on children's apps. You can read more information about Screen Time in the next chapter. Once you're done setting up Screen Time, you can tap on the Continue button and toggle on True Tone. You can adjust the size of your home screen icons using the Display Zoom. The iPhone 11 enables you to use gestures to navigate through your device.

Once you're done setting up your screen time, you can start using your device. The Apple user guide is always there for reference.

Chapter 7

Detailed Guidelines and Steps on How to Configure Your New iPhone 11

In the previous chapter, I gave a brief description of how to get started with your iPhone 11, including a brief step by step breakdown on how to set your passcode, perform data transfer, create a Face ID or Touch ID and more. In this chapter, I provide detailed steps and information about some of the initially discussed settings and how to make more advanced setups to improve your experience with your new iPhone 11 and get you started without much stress.

Setting Up Your Accessibility Option

With iOS 13, you can easily set up your accessibility option. You can easily zoom in for clarity using your iPhone 11 or any other iPhone running iOS 13. To zoom in, you need to enable zoom by tapping the screen twice with three fingers. Another option is to turn on the Voiceover feature to help you with the instructions if you have low vision. To set up the voiceover feature, press the side button three times and hold for the voice prompt indicating voiceover has been enabled. For models earlier than the iPhone X, you can use the home button instead of the slide button.

Other options that help you navigate through the process include:

The Display and Text Size, which gives you the flexibility to adjust text size, contrast and transparency.

Spoke Content reads all the text on your screen. You can also select the range of texts you want the speaking feature to catch.

Motion settings feature acts like the mouse sensitivity settings on a PC. Use this to reduce excessive user interface motion and to turn off message effects and video previews.

Touch Settings enables Assistive Touch and other Touch functionalities.

Switch Control is useful for highlighting screen elements that can be activated through an adaptive accessory.

The Keyboard configuration gives you a customized typing experience when you connect an external keyboard to your device.

Now, you can go back to setting up your accessibility options after tapping on the blue accessibility option.

How to Use the Quick Start

The QuickStart uses information gathered from your old iOS device to set up your new iPhone. You can then drop your content and data from iCloud backup into your new mobile device. Before you begin the process, please avoid the mistake most people make by continuing to use their old device while the QuickStart process is on, as they think only the new iPhone is affected. Quick-Start is on both devices when you trigger the transfer process, so ensure you pick a time when you won't need either mobile device.

Here are the steps to follow to set up your Quick Start:

Make sure your Bluetooth features are turned on and both devices are running iOS 11 and later, then turn on the new device and place them side by side or close to each other. The Quick start-up will load on your old iPhone and then prompt you to use your Apple ID in setting up your new iPhone. Sign in with the correct Apple ID and tap the continue button.

Once you sign in, some animation will appear on your new iPhone. Place your older iPhone over the new one and try to centre the animation on the screen in the viewfinder. You should get a message prompt that says Finish on your new iPhone. If you get an error message preventing you from using your old iPhone's camera, press the Authenticate Manually button and follow the next steps.

If stage 2 is successful, you will be asked to enter your old iPhone's passcode in your new iPhone. Once you're done with this, proceed to step 4.

Next, set up the Face ID on your iPhone 11. This step is straightforward; simply follow the step by step instructions to achieve the desired result.

You will be prompted to enter your Apple ID in the new iPhone. You will also have to enter the passcodes of your various Apple devices if you have more than one.

Once you've successfully entered the right Apple ID into your new iPhone, you have the option to restore information, including your apps, data and settings from your last iCloud backup. You also get the second option to update your older iPhone before restoring the data. To enable your new iPhone to pull data from the iCloud storage, make sure your Wi-Fi device is turned on. Then you can select a backup and filter how you want to transfer your settings, by Apple Pay, location and privacy.

Wait for the transfer to finish, and your new iPhone 11 will be updated with your previous settings and information.

Using the iPhone Migration for Direct Data Transfer

I'm sure you were excited when you heard about being able to use the QuickStart to set up your new iPhone 11, as long as your previous device runs on iOS 11 also. Well, if you want to transfer data between two phones with iOS 12.4 and above, there is more reason for you to get excited, as you can transfer data from your old phone to the new phone wirelessly or by connecting them. If the wireless network you are using for the transfer is slow or congested, you still have the option of choosing the wired method.

To use the wired method for your migration, you need the following: the Lightning to USB 3 Camera Adapter and the Lightning to USB Cable. The Lightning to USB 3 Camera goes into your old iPhone, while the Lightning to USB Cable goes into your new iPhone 11, and the other end goes into the adapter. Then plug the Lightning port of the Lightning to USB 3 Camera to a power source with at least 12 W supply.

Here is the step by step process to use the iPhone Migration:

Turn on your iPhone 11 and place it close to your old iPhone running iOS 12.4 or later. If you want to transfer the data using the wired connection, connect the wires as explained earlier. As usual, you will get the Quick Start screen that asks if you would like to use your old iPhone's Apple ID to set up your new iPhone 11. Enter the right Apple ID you intend to use and press the Continue button to proceed. If, after entering your Apple ID, you don't see the continue option on your old iPhone, check to see that the Bluetooth is on; if not, turn it on.

If the previous step is successful, an animation should appear after a while on your iPhone 11. Place your old iPhone over your new iPhone 11 and try to place the animation in the centre of the viewfinder. Wait for a moment and you will get message saying Finish on your iPhone 11. You might have issues using your old iPhone camera. Tapping Authenticate manually and following the proceeding steps will solve the problem.

Next, you should be prompted to enter a passcode on your new iPhone 11. You should enter the passcode for your old iPhone here.

Once you've entered the passcode successfully, you can now follow the instructions to set up your Face ID or your Touch ID on the new iPhone 11.

Now is the time to transfer your relevant data from your old iPhone to your new iPhone 11. So, choose the settings, such as Siri, Apple Pay and privacy settings, you want to transfer from your previous iPhone to the new iPhone 11.

While the transfer is going on, you will be prompted to answer if you would like to transfer data from any other device, such as an Apple Watch, into your new iPhone 11. So, use the opportunity to transfer all settings and data that you want to be updated on your iPhone 11.

Throughout the transfer process, you should keep both devices close together and do not forget to perform the data migration when you won't be needing either of the phones. To make sure both phones have adequate power to complete migration, it is advisable you connect them to a power supply, as the transfer process takes a considerable amount of time to finish.

Allow the transfer to finish and your migration is complete.

Chapter 8

Finishing Up Your iPhone 11 Settings

There are a few other settings you might need to do to complete your iPhone setup. After successfully migrating your data, you might have to re-enter your passcodes to your Mail App, Contacts and Calendar App.

To begin, go to Settings then open Password & Accounts.

Next, select each account and then enter your correct password when prompted.

Check Mail, Contacts and Calendar App

I would advise you to check if your Mail, Contacts and Calendar are up to date.

To begin, launch the Mail App and allow your emails to download to your new iPhone 11. Enter your email password when prompted to do so and proceed to set up your email.

For the Contacts App, once you open it, check to see that all your contacts from the previous iPhone were successfully transferred.

Next, open your Calendar App and check if all your events were successfully transferred. If not, you can use the iCloud to update your calendar events.

Enabling Notifications

In addition to the Mail, Contacts and Calendar apps, you might need to open other apps to enable their notifications. Once you open any app, when prompted, tap Allow Notification. If you open one and it does not allow notifications, you will have to do that from the settings. So, go to Settings and navigate to Notifications then open notifications for the app.

Bluetooth Accessories Pairing

Another setup you will want to do is pair your Bluetooth accessories, such as your speakers, Air Pods and headset. To do this, go to your Settings to open the Bluetooth and turn it on.

Now turn on any of your accessories that you want to pair with your iPhone 11 Bluetooth and put that accessory on Discovery Mode, then wait for the

accessory name to show up on your
iPhone 11.

Tap on the accessory name to pair it
with your iPhone 11 and enter your
passcode when prompted to do so.

Adding Your Credit/Debit Card to Apple Pay

For you to be able to use Apple Pay on
your new device, you have to add your
debit card, prepaid card, and credit
card to your Wallet.

To do this, go to your Settings and
navigate to Wallet & Apple Pay.

Tap on the plus (+) to add a new card.

Follow the instructions to enter your
card details and their security codes.
You may also need to download your
bank or card issuer's mobile app
before you can successfully add your
card to your wallet.

Once you have successfully entered the
correct details of your cards, your
bank service provider or card issuer
will run a check on the information
provided to verify your card. You
might be required to provide more

information or to input a confirmation code from your bank. Once you have the information, go back to your Wallet and tap on your card to enter the details.

Once the verification is done, tap next to complete the process. To add other cards, repeat the same process; you can add up to 12 cards on your iPhone 11.

Adding your card to Apple Pay makes payment easier with your iPhone, as your card can be used for payments on the Safari browser, and you can send money to family and friends using Apple Pay.

Managing Subscriptions

A subscription is what you pay to access content from a website or an app over an agreed period of time. For example, you can subscribe to Apple Music to get access to music of your choice, you can subscribe to Apple News+ for daily news updates, and you can subscribe to Apple TV channels, Apple Arcade and so on. Subscriptions are not limited to Apple, as you can subscribe to other third-party contents such as Spotify, Hulu, HBO Now and so on.

For most of these apps and other services, you have to pay a subscription fee by subscribing to a monthly or yearly plan for access to their content. Most times, once you link your cards to these subscriptions, they renew automatically until you cancel them. So now that you have linked your card to Apple Pay, you might want to manage those subscriptions.

Using the iCloud to Keep your iPhone 11 Calendar up to Date

The Calendar update is another advantage the iCloud offers iPhone users. With iCloud, your calendar is always handy. Changes made to your calendar update not only on your iPhone but on every device connected to that account. When you properly manage your events using your Calendar, you won't miss any appointments or meetings as you will be right where you need to be and when you need to be there. Here is how to perform default Calendar setting on your iPhone 11. Open your Settings and navigate to your Calendar, then choose from the list of options you want to make your Default Calendar. Note that when you create a new event, your iCloud will add this newly created event to your default calendar automatically. So, you should consider setting the Calendar you use the most as the default. You can also change your default calendar whenever you wish to. Just follow the previous steps to set up your default calendar. Once you are done setting up your default calendar from your mobile phone, the next thing you should do is make the same settings on your iCloud account. To do this, log on to iCloud.com and go to Calendar and locate the Settings icon. Next, open the Preferences and choose your preferred Default Calendar and tap on Save. With this, you can always make changes to your default Calendar settings using both your iPhone 11 and your iCloud account from any other device.

Managing Your Calendar Through Adding, Changing and Deleting an Event

Managing your calendar or schedule of events is easy and straightforward. Whatever changes you make using your iPhone will reflect on other devices immediately. To add an event, open your Calendar under settings and select the proposed date of the event. Tap on the plus sign and enter relevant information about the appointment or event. Editing a created event is as simple as creating the event. To do this, go to your Calendar and select the event you would like to edit. Update the event with the right information and save it. Having a lot of events can be distracting, as receiving constant notifications from events you aren't interested in can be annoying, especially when they occur frequently, like getting weekly reminders. To get rid of these unwanted events, open your Calendar and select the unwanted event and tap Delete Event. The Calendar only permits you to delete events you created. To remove events created by someone else, such as meetings, you have to Decline that event from the Invitation sent to you. Afterwards, you can remove that event from your calendar. Another tricky kind of notification or event to delete is subscriptions. Using the Calendar subscription is a handy way of staying up to date on current trends in sports, social media and so on. But like I stated initially, when this becomes too much, you might miss important event notifications. To delete a subscribed Calendar event from a social media website, such as Facebook, first you have to unsubscribe from that event. To unsubscribe from any Event on your iPhone 11, open your Calendar under Settings. Tap on the Calendars button and open the button with the information symbol. The information symbol is an "i" symbol with a circle round it ⓘ. You can then press the Delete Calendar to unsubscribe from the unneeded event. Once you have successfully unsubscribed from the event, you can then proceed to delete it from your Calendar by following the earlier steps to delete events from your iPhone 11 calendar.

Sharing Your Calendar with Family and Friends

With the Family Sharing feature, you can create a family group, like a social media chat group. But this feature functions to track your family members' schedules. Your family members are those who have been added to a group. Every family member can set appointments and can see everyone's schedules. Any changes made by a family member update automatically on every member's device in the group.

How to Change Your Time Zone

If you have a 3:00 p.m. event on your calendar and then you travel from San Francisco to New York, the event is going to alert you by 6:00 p.m. due to the three hours' time zone difference between San Francisco and New York. Your iPhone checks for your current time zone and automatically updates all your initially set events to align with that time zone. If you don't want this automatic update, you can override this in your iPhone 11 Calendar Settings.

To do this, launch your Settings and navigate to the Calendar. From here, locate and open the Time Zone Override then use the slider to turn on the Time Zone Override.

Once you are done, you can press the Time Zone button to get a list of the available Time Zones. Choose your preferred Time Zone and that's it! Your Calendar event will now retain its initial Time Zone and notifications will sound at the initially set time.

Managing Contacts on Your New iPhone 11

In this section, you are going to learn how to manage and delete contacts on your new iPhone 11.

- **Setting Up Your Contact Accounts**

The first thing to do is link your email accounts' contacts to the Contacts App. You can set up your contacts' accounts like your business directory.

First, open your Settings and tap on Password & Accounts. Then choose Add

Account, select your email account, and turn on Contacts. To add other contact accounts, like CardDAV and LDAP, tap on Other. Enter your details and password when prompted to do so then tap Next to finish.

- **Turning Accounts Contacts on or Off**

If you have set up an account and you want to remove the contacts, follow these steps to turn off the contacts.

Locate the Settings and choose Password & Accounts. Then choose the account with the contacts you intend to add or delete. For adding contacts, simply toggle the Contacts button On. If you want to remove contacts, simply toggle the Contacts button Off and press Delete Account to erase.

- **Setting Up Default Account for Adding New Contacts**

Since you can set up multiple accounts on your Contacts App, you can enjoy the ease of use if you choose a default account where you want your contacts to be saved. Follow these steps to choose a default account for your new contacts. Go to your Settings then open the Contacts and tap on the Default Account. This will bring up your contact accounts for you to choose your default contacts account.

- **Change How You Filter Through Your Contacts Display**

Here is another setting that can greatly improve the ease of use of your iPhone 11. This has to do with changing the way you sort your contacts alphabetically, using the last name or first name. To do this, open your Settings and choose Contacts. There are three options for you to choose from:

Option one is the Sort Order, which arranges your contacts based on the alphabetical order of the first name or last name.

Option two is the Display Order, which displays the first name of your contacts before or after their last names.

Option three is the Short Name, which enables you to sort how you want your contacts names to display in apps like Mail and Messages.

- **Deleting Contacts**

There are moments when you realize you have gathered a lot of contacts that were once relevant but have become a bit useless to you over time, and you want to delete them to make room for more. Before deleting your contacts, bear it in mind that they will be permanently deleted from your device, and anyone deleted from your email account will be deleted from all devices signed into that email. So, if you're sure you want to proceed, follow these steps. Go to your Settings and open the contact to be deleted, then tap edit and scroll downwards to the end of the page and tap on Delete Contact. If you are sure that's the contact you want to delete, you can tap Delete Contact again to confirm its deletion.

Effectively Using the Screen Time on Your iPhone 11

The Screen Time setting offers you the ability to access your activities on your mobile device in real-time, so you can view the weekly report on how much time you have spent on your iPhone 11. It offers you the leverage of setting time limits on mobile device usage. These settings come in handy when you feel you are beginning to slide down the slope of mobile usage addiction, especially when using fun apps such as games. Screen Time is not for phone owners only, as it gives parents the ability to set parental controls for their kids as well.

Using the Screen Time to know how much time you and your kids spend using your iPhone to navigate through fun apps and websites will go a long way in helping you make more informed decisions on your mobile phone usage principles.

To navigate to Screen Time, go to Settings and open the Screen Time tab. Turn it on and tap Continue to proceed. You will then have the option to select My Device or This is My Child's Device. There are two ways to create restrictions on your child's device. The first is to do that on their iPhone, while the second option is to do that through your own iPhone 11 using the Family Sharing Setting. The Family Sharing feature also enables you to view reports and tweak settings on your child's mobile device right from your own iPhone. To ensure you alone have access to changing the Screen Time settings, you can create a passcode to authenticate any changes, such as extending screen time. It is advisable you choose a passcode different from the one you use to unlock your phone.

To create a passcode for screen time, open your Settings and go to the Screen Time feature where you should see your child's name. Click on the child you want to adjust screen time setting and tap on the Change Screen Time Passcode to create a passcode. You will be required to authenticate the change using your Face ID, Apple passcode or your Touch ID. If you want to take off the Screen Time passcode, simply tap Turn Off Screen Time Passcode.

To use the Family Sharing feature, when you open your Settings, navigate to the Screen Time and open Set up Screen Time for Family. Follow the instructions provided to set up your Screen Time Family and add a child to your family. You can always add family members or children through the Family

Sharing feature. From your device, you can then get reports anytime you want and adjust the settings as required. Since you are in control, you can share music, games, movies and other apps that are safe for your kids.

The Screen Time provides a detailed report on your device usage, including apps opened and websites visited. To view this detailed report, go to Settings and open Screen Time, then Tap the See All Activity under the graphical representation. From here, you can get a quick glance of which apps you have used the most and decide if it is necessary to set a limit on that app. If you want to get information on all your devices that are signed in with your Apple ID, for example, if you want to view the report on your iPad using your iPhone 11, toggle on the Share Across Devices button.

There are four major settings you can adjust, including Downtime, App Limits, Content & Privacy Restrictions, and Always Allowed.

Downtime

Downtime is setting a time when you put all phone functions to a halt, except for phone calls and apps that you excluded from downtime. Downtime only has control over the apps for which you have enabled Screen Time. You will be given a five-minute notice before downtime begins and your screen time apps go to sleep.

App Limits

The App Limits helps you choose what app you want to limit. One good scenario is limiting gaming apps and social networking apps that limit your productivity. This could be done when you feel a sense of addiction to a gaming app within yourself or your kids, or you feel you need to be more productive at work, so you want to limit your chatting, tweeting and texting. By midnight every day, your App limit refreshes, and you can choose to extend or end the limits anytime you want.

Content & Privacy Restrictions

The Content and Privacy Restriction section is where you want to make the most adjustments if you would like to protect your kids from exposure to inappropriate content. With this, you have control over the kind of content that appears on your iPhone, and you can block downloads and prevent purchases. You don't want to be that mum who wakes up one day to see that her daughter just ordered a truckload of her favourite toys, using her card. So, the earlier you set those restrictions, the better.

Always Allowed

There are apps that you feel are always useful and you don't want them turned off for a moment. The Always Allowed feature helps you keep such apps functional, so you can always have access to them even when the downtime triggers on. These Apps will remain turned on even when you turn on the All Apps & Categories app limit. By default, the Phone Call, Phone Messages, FaceTime and Maps apps are always allowed, but you can choose to remove them.

Parental Control Tips for Your Child's iPhone

As explained in the Content & Privacy Restrictions section, you can limit app usage and protect your child from exposure to explicit content and making purchases with your phone. In this section, I provide steps to set content and privacy restrictions, prevent iTunes and App Store purchases, block explicit contents and prevent downloads.

How to Set Up Content and Privacy Restrictions on Your iPhone 11

To begin, open your Settings and go to Screen Time. Then tap on Continue. You will have to choose between My Device and This is My Child's.

If you're making changes from your child's device, choose the My Child's option and follow the instructions until you are prompted to enter and confirm the Parent Passcode. If you want to make restrictions using your iPhone, you can use the Family Sharing feature to restrict a family member. To prevent someone from changing your settings, create a Screen Time Passcode if you've not. Simply tap on the Use Screen Time Passcode to create a new one.

Once you're done with the previous step, open Content & Privacy Restrictions. Enter your password when prompted to do so then turn on the Content and Privacy button. Now that you've turned on the Content and Privacy, let's go through how you can manage some of the settings discussed earlier.

Preventing Purchases From the iTunes & App Store Purchases

This setting will help you prevent your child from making in-app purchases, installing unwanted apps or deleting any apps.

To begin, open your Settings as usual and go to Screen Time. Then tap on the Content & Privacy Restrictions button and enter your passcode if asked to do so.

Next, open the iTunes & App Store Purchases. You should get three Store Purchases & Downloads options. If you want to prevent your kids from installing apps, set the Installing Apps to Don't Allow, and if you want to prevent your child from making purchases, set the In-app purchases to Don't Allow, and the same goes for the

Deleting Apps settings. For the Required Password setting, you can choose to require a password for additional purchases by checking the Always Require button.

Preventing Explicit Contents

You can prevent your kids from exposure to explicit content, music and TV shows by filtering out contents with specific ratings.

To begin, go to your Settings and open Screen Time, navigate to Content & Privacy Restriction, and tap on the Content Restrictions. Then choose the type of content you would like to restrict.

Here is a breakdown of some of the contents you can restrict:

Ratings For: With this, you can select the approved rating for a country or region and apply those content ratings automatically.

Music, Podcasts & News: You can use this to filter out music, podcasts, and music videos containing inappropriate wordings and content for kids.

Apps: This will help you block apps that have a specific rating, such as violent games that are not appropriate for kids within a certain age range.

Music Profiles & Posts: This is where you can prevent your kids from seeing what their friends are listening to.

Other content restrictions include TV shows, Books and Movies, where you can stop them from reading books and watching movies and TV shows with certain ratings.

Adjusting Web Content Settings

The iOS 13 in iPhone 11 has been optimized to filter through your website content automatically and prevent access to adult content in your Safari browser and phone apps. You can also manage the settings to filter through it manually by adding a specific website you always want to allow.

Open your phone Settings, go to Screen Time and open Content & Privacy Restrictions.

Enter your Screen Time Passcode when prompted to do so and then tap on Content Restrictions.

Navigate to Web Content and open it. You have three options: to give Unrestricted Access, to Limit Adult Websites, and Allowed Websites Only.

If you want your iOS to filter out adult content automatically, check the Limit Adult Websites.

To enter specific websites that you want to prevent, check the Allowed Websites Only and use the Add Website button under the Never Allow section to prevent such websites.

Preventing Siri Web Search

Here is the final adjustment you might need to make pertaining to managing your web content.

Open your Settings and go to Screen Time. Then open the Content & Privacy Restrictions and tap on Content Restrictions. Navigate down to Siri and adjust the following settings.

The first is Web Search Content, which you should use to stop Siri from searching the web for answers when you ask a question.

The second is Explicit Language that you can turn off to prevent Siri from displaying any explicit language.

Restricting Gaming

With the improvement in processor power and GPU engines, iPhone 11 users are now open to many options when it comes to gaming. Playing games is good to help you relax, but when you begin to spend time gaming when you should be channelled into more productive ventures, then you need to start considering some forms of restriction. As adults, it is easier for us to say no to excessive gaming, but we know it is not the same for kids as they lack that same amount of willpower, so setting restrictions in gaming would go a long way in helping them stay focused.

To begin, locate the Screen Time feature under your Settings. Then go to Content & Privacy Restrictions and open the Content Restriction page. Navigate down to the Game Center to start making changes.

You can prevent any form of multiplayer games on the iPhone under the Multiplayer Games section.

Under Adding Friends, you can stop your child from adding friends to the Game Center.

You can also prevent game screen and sound recording, using the Screen Recording feature in the Game Center.

Chapter 9

Things to Do Before You Give Out Your Old iPhone

Before you get caught up in the euphoria of getting a new iPhone 11 and exploring the numerous features the new phone has, there are a few steps, guidelines you need to follow to sell, trade in, or give away your old iPhone properly. This is to ensure the safety of your information. In this section, I explain how you should go about removing your personal information from your old iPhone in a safe manner. Don't make the mistake of having to delete your information, such as your documents, contacts, calendars, photos, and videos, manually. Doing this manually while you are signed in to your iCloud account using your Apple ID will delete these files and data from the iCloud server, and you won't be able to access it on any device connected to that iCloud account. To erase your data securely, follow these steps.

Step 1

First, unpair your devices, such as your Apple Watch, from your old iPhone. You will find detailed steps on how to do that below.

Step 2

Once you have unpaired your devices, make sure you have backed up your device so that you have all your updated information on iCloud. You can find details on how to back up your device below.

Step 3

After successfully backing up your device, you can then sign out of iCloud and the iTunes & App Store.

If your device is running an iOS 10.2 or earlier, go to your iPhone Settings, open iCloud, and tap the Sign Out button. Press the Sign Out button again and tap Delete from my iPhone. You will be required to enter your Apple ID password for confirmation. Once you are done with iCloud, go to your Settings, open iTunes & App Store and tap on Apple ID, then tap on Sign Out.

For iPhone devices running iOS 10.3 or later, it's a much simpler procedure.

All you do is open your phone Settings and tap on Your Name. Navigate down and tap on the Sign Out button. Input your Apple ID password and tap on Turn Off, and you're done. You have successfully signed out of iCloud and iTunes & App Store.

Step 4

After signing out of iCloud and iTunes, you can erase your data securely. Go to your Settings and open General settings. Press Reset and tap on Erase All Content and Settings. You might be required to enter your Apple ID password if you have Find my iPhone turned on. You should be prompted to enter your device passcode. Once you do this, you can tap on Erase.

Step 5

You may contact your carrier to help transfer services to the new owner.

So, what if you have already given out your phone without performing the steps listed above? Well, there are things you can try to keep your data safe.

The first option is to contact the new owner of the phone and ask the person to follow the steps listed above to help erase the content.

Another method is for you to sign in to iCloud or Find My App using another device; you can use your new iPhone 11 for this. For this to work, your old iPhone should be connected to your iCloud and Find My App. Sign in to iCloud or Find My App on your new device, select the old device and tap on Erase. Once the process is done, choose Remove from Account to unlink the old phone from having access to your iCloud information.

If you cannot get in touch with the new owner of the phone and you don't have it on your iCloud and Find My App, you may choose to reset your Apple ID password. Changing your Apple ID password won't erase any of your personal information on the old device, but it will prevent the new owner of the old device from deleting contents from your iCloud.

If you are using the Erase All Content and Settings from the old iPhone as explained in the five steps of erasing your data, all iCloud services will be turned off and the information on your device will be erased completely. So, as well as your photo, music, apps, and contacts, it will also erase all your debit and credit card details that were added to your Apple Pay account, and this data wipe on your old device will not affect your iCloud content.

Now, if you are using Apple Pay on the old device and you were unable to do this erasure, you need to unlink your credit and debit cards from that device. To begin, launch iCloud.com and choose Settings. You should see a list of your devices connected to your iCloud. Choose the device next to Apple Pay and tap on Remove to unlink the device from your card.

How to Unpair Your Apple Watch from Your Old iPhone

Note that unpairing your Apple watch will restore it to factory settings.

To begin, place your old iPhone close to your Apple Watch. Then navigate to the Apple Watch app on your iPhone and tap on the My Watch tab.

Select the Watch you want to unpair by tapping on it then press the *ⓘ* to bring up the Watch information.

Press the Unpair Apple Watch button to take you to the next step.

If you're using the Apple Watch Series 4 or Series 3 with both GPS and Cellular connectivity, you should choose to keep your plan, since you might want to keep your plan.

Confirm your selection and enter your Apple ID password, and with that, you have successfully unpaired your Apple Watch from your iPhone.

Erasing Apple Watch

If you would like to erase your Apple Watch data, open Settings from your Apple Watch, go to General, and tap on Reset.

Next, choose Erase All Content and Settings and tap Erase All to confirm your selection.

Backing Up Your iPhone

Backing up your device saves a copy of your information so you can retrieve it when you want to switch to a new device due to replacement or loss of the previous device. Here are steps to back up your information using iCloud.

The first thing to do is connect to a good internet service, such as a Wi-Fi network.

Open your Settings and tap on Your Name under your profile picture. Navigate to the iCloud button and open it.

Once iCloud is open, toggle the iCloud Backup button on and tap the Back Up Now button.

Make sure you remain connected to a good network until the entire back up process is complete.

To confirm if the backup is complete, you can check the progress under the settings. Open your phone, Settings, and tap on Your Name. Then navigate to the iCloud page and tap on the iCloud Backup. On this page, you will find the date and time of your latest backup under the Back Up Now button.

Chapter 10

Using Face ID on Your iPhone 11

The face ID is a layer of security that helps you gain access to your iPhone and can be used to sign in to apps securely and authenticate purchases from Apple Store.

Before you begin setting up your Face ID, you should ensure that your TrueDepth camera is not covered by any particle and that nothing is covering your face. So, get rid of anything you normally won't be wearing on your face, such as caps and glasses. But if they are things you would normally wear, such as prescription glasses and contact lenses, it is okay to have them on as the Face ID has been designed to work with them.

Follow these steps to set up your Face ID:

Step 1

Open your iPhone 11 Settings and navigate to Face ID & Passcode.

Enter your passcode then tap on Set Up Face ID.

Step 2

Hold your iPhone at arm's length; about 10 to 20 inches from your face should do. You should be holding your phone in portrait mode, not landscape. (In case this part is confusing, portrait position means your phone is the longest top to bottom, while landscape means your phone is longest left to right).

After positioning your phone and your face correctly, tap the Get Started button.

Step 3

Try to adjust your face to fit within the circular frame and then begin to move your head slowly in a circular motion to complete the green circle around the frame.

If you are having any challenges moving your head, tap the Accessibility option for help.

Step 4

When you complete the motion, you should get a message saying First Face ID Scan Complete.

Tap the Continue button to proceed to the next stage.

Step 5

You will be required to repeat the Face ID scan for the second time, so move your head to complete the circle path. Once completed, you should get a message saying Second Face ID Scan Complete.

Step 6

Once you have completed the steps above, you will get a message saying Face ID is now set up. You can now tap Done to exit.

Now that your Face ID is set up, you can go to Face ID & Passcode under your phone Settings and choose what features you want to be authenticated with your Face ID, such as signing into apps and making purchases.

How to Unlock Your iPhone 11 Using your Face

Here are steps to unlock your iPhone using your Face ID.

Step 1

Wake up your iPhone by tapping on it or using Raise to Wake. Raise to Wake is a feature that automatically wakes the Lock Screen of your phone when you raise it. In case your Lock Screen does not come up when you raise your iPhone 11 to look at it, go to Settings, open the Display & Brightness configuration, and turn on Raise to Wake.

Step 2

Hold your iPhone 11 in portrait mode and glance at it. The Lock icon on your screen should animate from locked to open.

Step 3

You can now swipe upwards from the bottom of your screen to unlock it.

If you no longer want to use the Face ID screen to unlock, you can turn it off. Simply go to your Settings and navigate to Face ID & Passcode. Tap on the iPhone Unlocks to turn it off or on.

Using the Face ID to make online Purchases

Face ID can serve as a means of authentication when making purchases from the App Store and the iTunes store.

To make in-app purchases, follow the steps below.

Step 1

When you are done choosing your items from the app or website on Safari, check out and tap on the Buy with Apple Pay button. If the option is not available, choose Apple Pay as your method of payment and confirm the payment information before proceeding.

Step 2

If you want to use a different card than the default one, tap on the forward arrow ">" next to your card; if not, skip to Step 3.

Step 3

Now double press your iPhone 11 side button and glance at your iPhone screen (the side button is the button on the right side of your iPhone if you are holding your phone as you would normally to operate it). Your Face ID will be scanned, and you will get a message saying Done with a checkmark.

For purchases through the App Store, the iTunes Store and Book Store:

Step 1

To use the Face ID authentication on your iTunes and App Store, you need to ensure that iTunes and App Store are turned on as one of the features requiring Face ID authentication.

Step 2

When you are in your App Store, iTunes Store or Book Store and you find what you want to purchase, tap on the item to go to the payment page.

Step 3

When you are prompted to pay for the item, double press the iPhone side button.

Step 4

Glance at your iPhone screen and wait for the Face ID authentication to complete. You should get a message saying Done with a checkmark.

Signing in to Apps Using Face ID

Face ID can also be used as a security measure to have secure access to certain apps. For example, you can set up Face ID to authenticate usage of apps, such as your banking app and other phone apps that hold vital information. It can also be used to auto-fill username and passwords for websites on the Safari browser.

To set this up, follow these instructions:

Step 1

Open the app you want to use Face ID authentication with and tap on the sign-in button.

If prompted to use your Username and Password, select Allow the App to use Username and Password.

Step 2

Next, glance at your iPhone screen to sign in.

To check which Apps have been allowed to use Face ID, go to your Settings and navigate to Face ID & Passcode; open Other Apps to control which apps you want to use Face ID.

To use username and password autofill with your Face ID on websites in Safari, go to your Settings, navigate to the Face ID & Passcode, and turn on the Password AutoFill.

Now, to use this feature, load your Safari browser and visit the website you want to sign in to.

Tap on the sign in field to prompt you to enter your username and password, tap on it, and glance at your phone screen to autofill your username and password.

Chapter 11

Using Touch ID on Your iPhone 11

The Touch ID is another secure means of getting access to your device. Most people feel this is more convenient and less dramatic, since it uses fingerprint, rather than the Face ID that involves you glancing at your iPhone to gain access. Make sure you have created your passcode before you proceed to set up Touch ID.

Use the following steps to set up Touch ID for your iPhone:

Step 1

Wipe the home button clean using a smooth piece of paper and clean your finger, making sure there is no dirt or particle sticking on it.

Step 2

Go to your phone Settings and navigate to Touch ID & Passcode. Type your passcode when prompted to do so.

Step 3

Open the Add a Fingerprint button and press lightly on your iPhone home screen using your thumb preferably.

Step 4

Hold down your finger until you're asked to lift it or you feel the phone vibrate.

Step 5

Lift and place your finger slowly, changing the positioning of your finger slightly by tilting it to the right, left and so on, so the phone can capture a wider area of your finger.

Step 6

The last step involves adjusting your grip. To do this, hold your iPhone as you would when you want to unlock your phone. Then press your home button with the outer areas of your fingertip, rather than the centre of your finger that was first scanned.

Unlocking Your iPhone and Making Purchases Using Touch ID

Now that you have set up your Touch ID, it is time to use it to unlock your phone. To do this, press the home button with the finger you used to register for Touch ID.

Touch ID can be used in place of the Apple ID for authenticating purchases from the iTunes Store, App Store and Apple Books.

To make purchases with your Touch ID, follow these steps:

Step 1

Check to see if the iTunes & App Store is turned on by going to Settings and opening Touch ID & Passcode. If you have challenges turning it on, go to Settings, open iTunes & App Store, and sign in with your Apple ID.

Step 2

After turning on the iTunes & App Store feature, you can proceed to whichever store you want to make purchases from, including the iTunes Store, Apple Store or Apple Books.

Step 3

Choose whatever you want to buy by tapping on it; you should see the Touch ID authentication request pop up.

Step 4

To confirm the purchase, touch the home button lightly to capture your fingerprint.

With Touch ID, making a payment becomes easy as you can even make Apple Pay purchases from website stores on your Safari and Apps on your iPhone 11.

How to Manage Your Touch ID Settings

Managing your Touch ID settings from your iPhone 11 is quite straightforward. Go to your iPhone Settings and open the Touch ID & Passcode feature.

From here, you can see a list of features that would require your Touch ID authentication, such as the iPhone Unlock, the iTunes & App Store, Apple Pay and Password AutoFill. You can toggle the switch off to disable the Touch ID requirement for that feature.

You can also see a list of the fingerprints you have, as you can have up to five (5) fingerprints. You can rename a fingerprint by tapping on it to edit its name. To add another fingerprint, click on the Add a Fingerprint button and follow the instructions. But note that the more fingerprints you have, the longer your Touch ID fingerprint authentications will take. If you want to delete a fingerprint, all you would do is Swipe it to the bin to confirm the delete.

To identify a fingerprint from the list, touch your home screen button lightly as usual, and you will notice that the corresponding fingerprint is highlighted briefly.

With fast-paced technology growth, security is paramount when you're handling devices that hold your data and carry vital information, so you should make conscious effort to safeguard yourself and your data. That is why I've taken the time to explain how to secure your iPhone 11 within these last few chapters. With that, I believe you know all you need to know to have exclusive access to your new iPhone 11. In the next chapter, we will discuss some tips and tricks you can implement to have a better experience with your iPhone 11.

Chapter 12

Tips, Tricks and Updates to Help You Enjoy Your New iPhone 11

Here, we are going to look at some of the new features that come with the iPhone 11 iOS 13 and how you can utilize them to get the best experience with your new iPhone 11.

Adding a Virtual Home Button

Any previous iPhone user will admit that, prior to the release of the new iOS 13, it was almost impossible to imagine using an iPhone without the home button. The expulsion of the home button from the iPhone 11 might startle iPhone users, as most of us cannot imagine our lives without it. It is like Apple has literally taken away our home because we are used to pressing the home button when we seem to have come to the end of our adventures and don't have the time to start closing every page or app we open. Now that we no longer have a home button, how do we go home? Well, the answer to this is the use of gestures, and you will enjoy your new iPhone 11 better if you know how to use these gestures, as there are so many gestures for different actions. In the next chapter, we will run through some of the gestures that you should know to get the best experience with your iPhone 11. But for now, let us focus on how to add our virtual home button.

To do this, open your Settings and scroll down to Accessibility. When you open Accessibility, scroll down to the PHYSICAL AND MOTOR tab, where you will see the feature called Touch. Tap on it and when it opens, tap on the Assistive Touch button. It should be set to Off by default. Toggle on the button to enable the Assistive Touch, and with that, you should see a digital home button appear at the bottom of your screen.

With this, you can perform all the functions of the usual home buttons in previous versions of Apple iOS. You can click on it wherever you are on your phone, and it will take you back to your Home Screen. You can access the Control Panel from your virtual home button, and you can even enable Siri and access your notifications from there.

Another special functionality the virtual home button offers over the usual home button is that you can move it to somewhere more comfortable. To do this, simply press the virtual home button and drag it to wherever you want it then release your finger to drop it right there.

The New Dark Mode

These days, we spend a lot of time on our mobile devices. We are texting, chatting on social media channels, replying to emails, playing games and so on. A lot of applications or platform providers are beginning to leverage on our need for easy accessibility to their apps and services. Therefore, they are building mobile versions of their applications to keep us engaged. All these apps increase the time we spend staring at our mobile phones, and there are times when you just want to give your eyes a break. The new dark mode is the perfect feature to help you relieve your eyes from excessive screen brightness.

There are a couple of ways you can turn on the Dark Mode for your iPhone 11. The first one is to go to your phone Settings and open the Display & Brightness section. Under the appearance setting, you will see the light and dark mode with sample images on how your phone would display when you apply either of the effects. Tap on the dark mode to turn it on and watch your iPhone turn from the usual light screen background to a dark background right there within the Settings page.

Another way you can set the dark mode for your iPhone 11 is through the Control Center. To bring this up, swipe down from the top right corner of your iPhone 11. Tap on the dark and light mode icon to switch between dark and light mode for your iPhone.

Another way to turn on dark mode is to ask Siri. To do this, you need to get Siri to listen to you by pressing on the side button, as usual. You can then say, 'Turn on Dark Mode'. If you are having challenges using this feature, you read the instructions on how to set up Siri. If this is successful, you will get a reply from Siri saying "Ok, I turned on Dark Mode", and of course, your iPhone should now be in dark mode. When you want to revert to light mode, you can repeat the same process by pressing your side button and telling Siri to turn off dark mode.

What makes the dark and light mode so attractive is how it affects the wallpaper display. The four new wallpapers that come with the new iOS 13 integrate seamlessly with the light and dark mode like they were specifically designed to bring out the best of the dark/light mode feature. In addition to the four new wallpapers, the dark mode affects other wallpapers as well, and you can dim their brightness when the dark mode is turned on.

Another thing that makes the dark mode so cool is how it affects your Apps and their display. It gives them such a powerful yet comfortable feel. For example, your calendar and notes interfaces totally change like they were upgraded with new interface design. Some third-party software, like twitter, has also updated their applications to support dark mode.

For the best effect, try using the dark mode at night or when you're in a dark or dimly lit room. You will feel a lot more relief on your eyes.

The 3D Map Feature

This is probably the greatest addition to the list, as there are some cool things you can do with maps on your iPhone 11. To enjoy the new 3D map, open the Maps app on your desktop and tap on any part of the city you want to view. Now tap on the Map Settings button, which is the topmost icon on the top right corner of the map app. From the Map Setting page, open the Satellite tab. Now tap on the 3D icon, which is the last element on the top right corner of the screen. From the 3D map view, you can pan around using two fingers; you can zoom in and rotate to look around. The 3D view gives you a realistic view that is quite laudable compared to the google maps street view. With this, you will get a better understanding of the terrain you're currently in or about to visit.

The 3D view is not the only change that makes the updated map so amazing. Another great feature of the map is the Look Around feature. This gives you a virtual reality sort of walk around the area you're currently viewing.

To activate this view, place a pin on the area you want to view. The Marked Location page should pop up above the map. Tap on the Look Around button, and you will be given an immersive experience of the location you picked. Another way to open the Look Around feature is to tap on the binoculars icon whenever you see it on your map. The Look Around feature gives you a 360 view of your location. To move to a landmark, such as a restaurant, you can just tap on that point, and the map will zoom in to the point. You can also get more information about that restaurant, such as their menus and business details. At the time of writing this book, the functioning of the Look Around feature is currently limited to some states in the US, but Google is working to make it available throughout the US and other countries of the world.

Changing Contact Information in Message

With the changes in iOS 13, you can change your iPhone 11 contact information to determine how other iPhone users see your details when you are chatting with them.

To make these adjustments, open your Settings and scroll down to the Messages button and open it.

Tap on the Share Name and Photo feature to start making changes. From here, you can change your photo and name.

To change your picture, tap on the photo avatar, and you have the option of choosing from a list of Animoji's and taking or uploading your own picture.

Going back to the name and photo options, you can toggle on the Name and Photo Sharing option to allow your Messaging app to share your contact details. You have two options for sharing your information. You can decide to share your information to your contacts automatically by checking the Contacts only tab or set it to always ask by checking the Always Ask.

Ability to Use Some iPhone Features on Other Apple Devices

The iPhone 11 gives you the ability to perform some of its functions, such as receiving a phone call, on other compatible Apple devices, like your Mac. This feature is great for performing relevant tasks that would normally require you to use your phone when your iPhone is not handy. Imagine you've left your iPhone in the bedroom and you're somewhere else, like in your sitting room, working with your laptop, and your phone suddenly rings. Instead of abandoning your position and breaking your workflow by walking to the bedroom, you can easily pick up your call using your MacBook.

To leverage on this feature, open your Settings and tap on the Phone button. Open the Calls on Other Devices page.

Toggle on the Allow Call on Other Devices button and then choose from the options by toggling them on.

To receive messages on other devices as well, go to your Settings and open Messages. Tap on the Text Message Forwarding button to display the devices you can toggle on to receive or send text messages.

Enhanced Privacy Settings

As we all know, Apple is a company that takes data privacy seriously, and they are always trying to stay on top when it comes to designing systems with high-end security measures.

With the new iOS 13 and iPhone 11, they have taken the data privacy of their customers to a whole new level. With this iPhone, users can force Apps to request their permission to access their location. To enable this new feature, go to your Settings and open Privacy. Tap on the Location Services to see a list of apps using your location. To make an App request permission rather anytime it wants to use your location, enable the Ask Next

Time feature. This extra option is an addition to the two options of Never and While Using the App, which either stops the app from accessing your location when setting to Never or always accessing your location when setting to While Using the App.

Most iPhone users don't know this, but there are some apps that are constantly using your Location feature to track you without you knowing it. Another way this is done is through Bluetooth, where you have some apps using your location information when you allow them access to your Bluetooth. So, when you want to share a photo, you can turn off the Location information before sending the picture.

In previous chapters, I explained how you should erase all your data before transferring your old iPhone to another user. If you are a security-sensitive individual and would like to keep your information private, you might want to consider turning on the Erase Data feature. How this works is, when you turn this feature on and there are up to 10 failed attempts to unlock your iPhone 11, all your iPhone data will erase.

To use this feature, open your Settings, Tap on Face ID & Passcode, and enter your Passcode when prompted to do so. Scroll down to the bottom of the list. You will see the Erase Data feature. Toggle the button on to enable it.

I would advise you to make sure you've backed up your data on iCloud before doing this. You can go through the steps on how to back up your data in previous chapters.

The last thing we will talk about in this section is the ability for you to prevent unknown callers from distracting you. This feature is called the Silence Unknown Callers; it can be very useful when you want to keep your privacy. The world is a global village and even though some websites and applications promise data privacy when you use their application, not all keep that promise. So, maybe you've filled a form online and have given out your phone number and you begin to receive unsolicited phone calls from telemarketers, scammers, stalkers, spam callers and even wannabe boyfriends. Go to your Settings and tap on the Phone icon, and under the CALL SILENCING AND BLOCKING CONTACTS, you can toggle on the Silence Unknown Callers to save yourself from unnecessary disturbance.

New Document Scanner

If you play around with files and documents, then you are going to love this new iPhone 11 scanning feature. You can access this scanner through your Files app on your desktop. Click on the Files app and tap on the Browse button at the bottom right corner of the screen. On the Browse page, you will see three dots at the top right corner of your screen; tap on it to open the options available. Select the Scan Documents button and place any document you want to scan in front of your camera behind your phone. Your iPhone will then try to detect the document you want to scan. When you see the coloured highlight has covered the area you want to scan as closely as possible, tap on the round button to capture your image. Now you can move the anchor points to fit your image properly in the scan area, and once you're satisfied, click on Keep Scan to scan the document. To make edits, tap on the scanned image. From here, you can add the black and white filter to make the image look more like it was scanned using a scanning machine.

Saving Battery Life

The new iPhone 11 comes with upgraded battery life, but here is a setting you can adjust to improve your battery life, called Optimized Battery Charging. One thing that reduces the longevity of batteries is excessive charging and this is because some people plug in their charger and then leave it to charge throughout the night. When you do this, your iPhone charges up to 100 per cent, and your mobile phone keeps receiving power supply. The Optimized Battery Charging learns your charging routine. So, when you plug in your iPhone, it charges up to 80 per cent and then waits until about the time you will need your iPhone before it charges the remaining 20 per cent.

Exploring the New Animoji and The Updated Memoji

With the update on iOS 13, the iPhone 11 comes with three new Animoji characters, the mouse, the octopus and the cow. These Animojis track the movement of your face and then try to emulate those expressions. The Memoji has been updated with extra facial features, such as additional hairstyles, eyebrows, piercings and earrings. You will also gain access to a lot more Animoji and Memoji stickers. Stickers are a way to make your chat more fun and engaging, and they go a long way in adding more meaning to your messages. Texting does not offer that facial expression you get when communicating face to face with someone. Dragging a sticker into your message can help translate your mood to the recipient. One other cool thing about the updated Animoji and Memoji is that you can access them even outside your messaging app, such as your Notes. Just open your Memoji tab to access them.

The New Quick Path Typing

Here is another amazing feature the new iOS 13 is offering iPhone 11 users. With this feature, you don't need to download any third-party apps to swipe through your keyboard while typing. If you don't know about this swipe typing feature or you've not used it, it is straightforward and comes in handy when you don't feel like tapping on your phone keyboard. To use this feature, simply think of a word you want to type and place your finger on the first letter of that word. Now, slide your finger across the screen in a path that would cut across every letter in that word. You can start with short words to get comfortable doing this before moving on to more complex statements. The good thing about this is that there is no setting for this, so you do not have to turn off the keyboard tapping to use keyboard swiping; you can use both interchangeably.

Another extra typing tip I would like to offer you, in case you don't know how to use it yet, is the easy text selection. If you are typing and you want to copy or cut out one word, simply double tap on that word to highlight it for copying. If you want to select a whole sentence, triple tap on any word within that sentence. To select an entire paragraph, all you need to do is quadruple tap.

Upgraded Safari Download Manager

If you are familiar with the Safari browser for any of the previous iPhones running on any iOS less than iOS 13, you know the Safari Download feature is anything but user-friendly. When you click on the download button for iOS 13, you don't get any confirmation to begin downloads. But for the iOS 13 on the iPhone 11, you will get pop-up information about the file you want to download, and you have to press the download button once more to approve the download. A download manager has also been added to the Safari browser. To access this, tap on the download icon at the top right corner of your phone screen when you are in the downloads page. From here, you can also open the downloads folder by tapping on the magnifying glass icon.

You can also change the downloads folder by going to Settings, opening the Safari button, and tapping on the downloads. By default, it should be set to save on iCloud, but you can pick a folder in your local drive to save your downloads.

Using the App Action

Another feature to make life easier for iPhone 11 users is a simple feature that lets you get a preview of quick actions you can use with your apps. To use this feature, you just have to press on the app of your choice to get a list of things that app can do for you, then you can select one action, and once the app loads, it will take you right into that section of your app. Let's take, for example, the Instagram app. When you press on the icon, you will get a list of Instagram functions: the Camera, New Post, View Activity and

Direct. Rather than opening Instagram and starting from the home page, you can jump right to the Camera function.

Purging Multiple Tabs

There are people who love to keep things simple by opening one tab at a time and closing it immediately after they are done, and there are the special ones who are always multitasking. They can open as much as 20 tabs on their Safari browser; it could be a list of items they want to shop online, articles they want to read and so on. What happens is, over time, these pages begin to accumulate, and you probably have no need to return to most of those pages even if you intended to do so in the first place. Before you realize this, you might have up to 10 or 20 pages that you would have to hit the X button to close them. With this feature, you can program your iPhone 11 to purge these webpages within a specific time interval.

To use this feature, go to your Settings and scroll down to Safari. Navigate down to the TABS section, where you will see the Close Tabs. By default, it should be set to Manually. Go in and change it from Manually to either the After One Day, After One Week, or After One Month option depending on which one you feel comfortable with.

Ability to Edit Videos and Photos Better

With iOS 12 on previous versions of the iPhone, you don't get many editing options for your videos and photos. For video editing, you can only trim the videos to the desired start and end time. But with the iPhone 11's new iOS 13, we have an almost endless list of video editing opportunities for you to try. You can trim by adjusting the play backslider when you are in the editing mode. You can add filters and effects, such as noise reduction, highlights, shadows, contrasts, intensity, tint and vignette. You can make other adjustments, such as modifying the video's aspect ratio and changing its orientation.

Another feature is the ability to embed your video edits data in your video whenever you want to share it with your friends. This metadata enables your friends to see your original videos and all the edits you have made when you share your video with them. This makes it easier to collaborate with your friends when you all want to edit a video together using your iPhone 11. To enjoy this feature, go to your Send options and toggle on the All Photos Data.

Something for the Mobile Game Lovers

The introduction of the Apple Arcade for iOS 13 has offered mobile game lovers a reason not to look elsewhere to satisfy their gaming fantasies. There are many great games with great qualities that you can play and are quite affordable at $5 per month.

Another interesting update is the PlayStation and Xbox controllers support for the Arcade on the iOS 13 platform. With this, you get the flexibility and comfort that desktop games offer, while you're playing on your iPhone 11.

Saving Up Your Data

There are times when you have limited data, and when you don't manage that, you might end up running out of data. There are times when you might have to leave your comfort zone, where you have unlimited data supply, to go someplace where you are on a metered data usage. For example, you might go on vacation and you won't have access to unlimited data usage. To manage your data, you might need to check some apps silently consuming your data in the background. The iOS 13 comes with a new feature that helps you with this. Activating a metered or low data usage mode helps to conserve your data greatly.

To access this feature, go to your phone Settings and tap on Cellular. Here you should see the cellular data option. Open it and toggle on the Low Data Mode option.

Fast Emergency Dialing

No one expects or hopes to be in an emergency where they need urgent and timely help. As we all know, no matter how safety conscious we try to be, there are some situations we cannot control. That is why you need to put measures in place to salvage such unprecedented events. In any emergency, every second matters and timely action is required. So, although we don't hope to be in that condition, we need to put measures in place just in case the unexpected happens.

By default, the emergency and power off feature are triggered on when you press the side button and any of the volume buttons simultaneously. But you have to hold it much longer for it to activate the emergency SOS and dial emergency service.

There is another way that is faster, as it only triggers emergency and not both emergency and power off.

To access this feature, go to your Settings and open the Emergency SOS page. Toggle the Call with Side Button on to activate this command. With this, all you would do is press the side button five (5) times to trigger on the Emergency dial. Turning on this feature won't affect the other option of pressing the side button with any of the volume buttons, as you can use either of the two. But I highly recommend you turn on this button, as it is not only more specific to the Emergency SOS, but it is also faster to turn on. You just need to press it 5 times.

Once you've toggled on the Call with Side Button, it is time for you to set up your emergency contacts. This step is just as important as turning on the emergency button.

You can set up your Emergency SOS contacts in your Medical ID using the Health app.

To begin, go to the Emergency SOS and locate the Setup Emergency Contacts in Health tab, tap on the button to open, and follow the instructions.

Usually, you would add some emergency contacts to your list of emergency contacts; this could be the family doctor, your spouse, your mum or your dad, and even friends you believe could provide adequate help. Once you trigger on the emergency dial by pressing the side button five times, messages are sent to your list of

Emergency SOS numbers, and these messages carry your location so help can be provided immediately.

Remember, it is better to be safe than sorry at the end of the day. So, make sure you toggle on the button and ask your family members and friends to do the same.

Using the Hidden Track Pad

Just like the Quick Path, this is another amazing feature that iOS 13 users are going to like, especially if you are going to be doing a lot of typing using your new iPhone 11. To understand how important this feature is, imagine how frustrating it is when you are typing then you realize you need to make corrections, then you start trying to place the cursor right on the letter you want to delete but then you keep missing the positioning by a letter. With this trackpad, you can easily slide your cursor around until you get to where you want to make corrections.

To use this feature, all you do is press down on your Space Bar when you are texting, and you should see your keypad area greyed out. Start moving your finger around to move the trackpad to where you want it to be.

Taking Full Page Screenshot with Your iPhone 11

If you want to screenshot a webpage, we all know how simple and straightforward this is. All you do is press on the side button at the same time as the up-volume button, and your screenshot will be taken, very easy, right? But how about when almost everything on the webpage is relevant and you want to capture it all? For previous versions of iOS, you would have to take one screenshot, save it, and then scroll down to take another and keep repeating the process, depending on how bulky the webpage content is.

But with the new iOS 13 on iPhone 11, there is a new feature called the Full Page that can take screenshots of the entire webpage. Here is how to use it.

Press down the side button with the upper volume button as you would normally do to take a screenshot. Now when your iPhone has taken the screenshot, tap on the screenshot image to take it to the editing mode. From here, you will see a couple of editing features, like annotating your image, highlighting and drawing on it, but those are not what we are looking for. What we need is at the top right corner of the page, and that is the Full Page button.

Tap on it and your iPhone will capture screenshots of the entire webpage in sequence just as it is on the website. You can now do whatever editing you want, and when you're done, tap on the Done button at the top left corner of the screen to save it on your drive.

Using the Upgraded Reminders App

Looking at the old reminder app of the iOS iPhone versions and comparing it with the newly designed reminders app of iOS 13, you can see there was a total overhaul of the reminder app, as the previous design just looked bland. The UI was redesigned to fit more into a modern-day app interface. But the reminders app revamp was not only about better design; it was also about better functionality. When it comes to staying organized, the new reminder app offers you the best possibilities. You can create your own list when you open your Reminder App by tapping on the Add List at the bottom right corner. You can easily add some customization by adding your own colours, avatar and name.

In any of the lists, you can add your reminders by tapping on the New Reminder button at the left corner of the List you chose. You can use the quick toolbar to add some parameters to your activity. Clicking on the clock button icon enables you to add when the Reminder should alert. You can also click the □ icon to have more options. Take some time to explore the various options.

To help you stay more organized, you can create subtasks under a parent reminder. Here is an example of how best to use this feature. Let's say it is a weekend and you have a lot of things you want to do. You want to rush to the grocery store, your daughter needs to go to her dance class, you need to take her to the dentist after that, your son wants to go to his football practice, while you need to drop by work briefly to finish up some specific tasks.

If I was to organize this using the subtask feature, I would create three-parent reminders and name them something like: Take Care of Kids, Go Grocery Shopping and Office Priorities.

Now I would create the tasks: Pick Up Daughter from Dance Class, Take Daughter to Dentist, Pick Up Son from Football Practice. Then I would make them all Subtasks of Taking Care of Kids.

For Go Grocery Shopping, I would have: Eggs, Milk, Veggies, Meat, Butter and so on. The Office Priorities would have tasks I must complete, ensuring that the short time I spend at work is worthwhile. I believe you get the entire picture. With this method, you can minimize your subtasks and just have those three parent reminders, and when you want to, you can maximize to view them.

To make a reminder a subtask of another reminder, simply hold and drag the subtask into the parent reminder. When a parent reminder has been created, you can hold and slide any reminder below it to the right to indent it into a subtask.

To help you stay even more organized, besides grouping Reminders within a List, you can also group Lists into a Folder. To do this, simply drag a List into another List to create a new group.

Chapter 13

Doing Things Faster on Your iPhone 11 Using Gestures

As I explained earlier, in this chapter, I will explain how you can achieve some functionalities by using some gestures. In the previous chapter, I showed you how you can bring up the virtual home button, so here I will explain how to use gestures to go home, switch between apps, invoke Siri, your Control Panel and so on. The gestures for iOS 13 have been greatly improved, so whether you're a new iPhone user or a veteran user, you might still need some help understanding some of the new gestures.

Image Credit: Mothership.sg

Going back to Your Home Screen

To go back to your home screen from wherever you are on your iPhone 11, from the gesture area at the bottom edge of your screen, swipe your finger up your phone display. If you are not a new iPhone user, you should find this gesture to be quite like how you would normally bring up the Control Center. Now that we know how to return to the home screen from any point on our iPhone, we can explore other functionalities without fear of not being able to find our way home.

Switching Between Apps on Your iPhone 11

On earlier versions of the iPhone, you would have to bring up the fast app switcher for you to swipe from one app to the other on your iPhone. With the new iPhone 11 and the iPhone XS, all you do is swipe right, and you swiftly move between apps. Most times, this should work smoothly, but some older apps might have glitches, so try to run an update on all apps to their latest versions. To switch apps, place your finger on the gesture area at the bottom of your iPhone screen and swipe left to right or from right to left.

Swiping from left to right takes you back to previously opened apps, while the right to left swipe takes you to more recently opened apps. This means that, once you stop, the last app you opened will be your most recent app, and you can only swipe backwards.

Using the Fast App Switcher for Multitasking

If the basic swiping is not efficient for you to move between apps, then the fast app switcher would provide you with more flexibility and help you stay organized. It also makes it easier to close apps you no longer use. If you're an old iPhone user, who is not used to iOS 13, you might think all you have to do is double-tap the home button or use the 3D touch swipe to bring up the fast app switcher, but these methods will not to work, but there is a gesture to bring up your multitasking interface.

To use the gesture, touch the gesture area at the bottom of your iPhone 11 screen with your finger then swipe up gently and pause. You don't have to swipe completely to the top of your screen, just a short way up, and it should work. You also don't have to swipe fast like you want to flip; this would take you to the home button. Try it a few more times and it will become second nature. It's quite simple. Slide up gently, pause for a moment, and your fast app switcher will pop up.

Once you are in the fast app switcher, you can easily purge any apps you no longer want open. To do this, simply swipe up on any app you want to close, and it'll be gone. You can also close multiple apps by placing a finger on each app and then swiping them all up to close.

Entering Reachability Mode

This is one important feature that some mobile phone users are not taking advantage of. Whether you are new to the iPhone or a veteran iPhone user like some of us, this is one feature you should be able to use at appropriate moments. If you're still wondering what reachability mode is all about, it simply brings your iPhone closer to your fingers, so they can reach it easily. Most times, when you want to be very efficient with your phone, you need to operate it with both fingers, but there are times when you are tired or in bed and you simply want to operate your iPhone with only one hand. If you feel you are never too tired to operate your phone and won't be needing the reachability mode, consider the time you spend leaving your toothbrush hanging in your mouth while brushing your teeth and trying to perform task on your iPhone with both hands.

The reachability feature comes in handy at such moments, as you can keep going up and down with your toothbrush on one hand, and your finger, on the other hand, can go all over the place on your minimized iPhone 11 display.

To use this gesture, you need to set it up first. To begin, open your Settings and tap on General, then open the Accessibility and navigate to Reachability. Toggle the button on to activate reachability. Once you are done setting it up, place your finger on the gesture area at the bottom of your screen and swipe downwards to open reachability.

Staying in Control with the Control Panel

For users who are not new to the iPhone, you will find the multitasking gesture to be similar with how you would usually open the control panel in older iPhone versions. With iOS 13, things have changed a little, so to open your Control Panel, your finger should be placed on the top right corner of your iPhone display and swipe down.

Opening Notifications

The gesture for opening your Notifications is like that of the Control Panel, only instead of swiping from the top right corner of your iPhone display, you have to swipe from the top left corner. If you're wondering how far is right or left when swiping from the top, you can use your iPhone notch as the demarcation.

Chapter 14

Getting the Best out of the Improved iPhone 11 Camera

The most notable feature the iPhone 11 comes with is its upgraded camera. According to Apple, the iPhone 11 features a next-generation Smart HDR that recognizes people and improves their appearance by producing natural-looking skin tones and adding the necessary highlights and shadows.

Image Credit: Flickr.com

Another feature of the iPhone 11 camera that I will discuss using is Night Mode. The iPhone 11 Night Mode is designed to give you a better lit photo in low light. This feature is possible due to the larger sensor of the wide-angle camera that has 100 per cent Focus Pixels. When you take pictures in an area with poor lighting, the Night Mode comes on automatically, so you don't need to use your flashlight.

The ability to take Portrait Mode is another great ability of the iPhone 11. The portrait mode photo focuses on the main subject and blurs out the background, like the bokeh effect you get using the DSLR camera. Comparing the portrait mode of the iPhone XR with that of the iPhone 11, you will notice there has been a great improvement; the iPhone XR portrait mode only recognizes people and applies the bokeh effect, but with the iPhone 11, you can focus on almost any object, like your car, your food or even your dog, and blur out the environment. The iPhone 11 also gives you the ability to move the lighting effects of your photos around using portrait lighting. The iPhone 11 also supports more lighting modes, such as the Stage and Stage Mono, than the iPhone XR.

How to Use the Night Mode Feature

The amount of light entering your camera sensor is measured in the luminance metric (lux), and Apple has designed the Night Mode to work in environments around 10 lux. When you are in a dark environment, the luminance metric is about 100 lux, and during twilight or in a poorly lit room, the lux value falls between 10-15 lux value. Once the lux value is below 10, the Night Mode will come up automatically, but if the lux value of the environment is not so low, the Night Mode will be suggested if the environment is dark. This will appear at the top left of your iPhone 11 screen in the shape of a crescent moon. If you feel the night mode would be necessary, simply tap on the button to toggle it on, and it will turn yellow.

Once the Night Mode is enabled, you can press down on the shutter button and hold it still for your camera to simulate the long exposure. The camera Night Mode automatically simulates a long exposure from 1 to 3 seconds, depending on the lux value of the environment, so if you feel the automatic value it sets for you is not going to give you the best quality, you can always adjust it up to a maximum value of 10 seconds using the slider under the viewfinder.

If you ever feel you don't want the Night Mode when using your camera, you can always toggle off the yellow Night Mode button.

How to Take "Slofies" Using Your iPhone 11

With the new iPhone 11 updates, you can now take "slofies", which is a slow-motion video at a frame rate of 120. The word slofie was invented by combining the word slo-mo and the word selfie. Another feature of the upgraded 12-megapixel front camera is the ability to take a wider shot by flipping the phone landscape. This capability is ideal for group selfies.

To take your slow-motion selfie, follow these steps:

Step 1: Launch your iPhone camera.

Step 2: Tap on the perspective flip button under the viewfinder, which is the button on the right side of the big shutter button. This will activate the front camera.

Step 3: Next, you should select the Slo-Mo option by swiping through the shooting mode options until the 'Slo-Mo' option is centred on the screen right above the shutter button.

Step 4: Tap on the shutter button to record your slow-motion picture, and when you're done, tap on the shutter button once again to end the slofie.

Shooting Videos Fast Using the iPhone 11 QuickTake Feature

You can quickly switch from taking photos to making a video with the improved camera feature. To make videos on previous iPhone versions, you would have to go into the options to select video if you're in photo mode.

So you're taking photos and you want to switch from photo mode to video mode on your iPhone 11. Simply press down on the shutter button while making your video and let go once you're done to end the recording.

If you want to continue recording without having to hold the shutter button, slide the elastic button to the far right and place it on the padlock icon to lock it in place. In this position, you can even take still photos by tapping on the white shutter button. When you are done with your QuickTake, tap on the red record button to end it.

Taking Burst Photos with iPhone 11

To take a series of pictures rapidly at 10 frames per second, you should try the burst mode.

Press the shutter button and drag it to the far left until the elastic shutter is on the last picture you took. Hold the finger in place, while the camera takes a series of images. You will notice a counter increasing on the original shutter position. This indicates the number of photos taken. Once you're satisfied with the number of photos taken, let go of the shutter button.

With these few tips on how to make the most of your camera, I will sign out on this elaborate guide on how to get started with your iPhone 11. I believe I have covered all you need to know to enjoy your new iPhone 11. If there are any parts you think I have missed and would want me to cover, please don't hesitate to drop a message in the review section. I would love to work with your feedback. Now that you know how powerful your iPhone 11 is, you can wield it with confidence. So, go out there, get creative, and don't be afraid to explore other features.

www.ingramcontent.com/pod-product-compliance
Lightning Source LLC
LaVergne TN
LVHW022321060326
832902LV00020B/3597